Reader's Digest
Wildlife Watch

Grassland & Woodland in Autumn

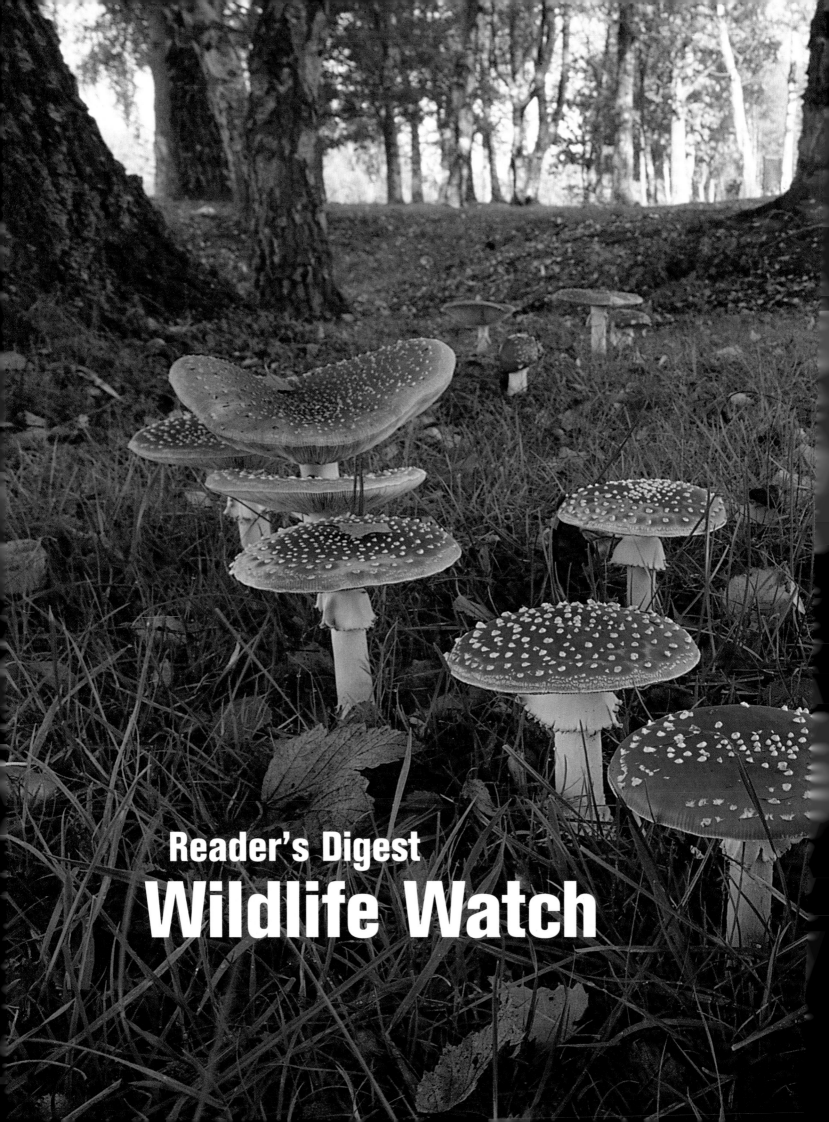

Reader's Digest
Wildlife Watch

Grassland & Woodland in Autumn

Published by
The Reader's Digest Association Limited
London · New York · Sydney · Montreal

Contents

Wildlife habitats and havens

12 Bramble patches

16 Ancient green lanes and tracks

20 In and around an old beech tree

24 The larch forest

28 Woodland after dark

32 The New Forest – mosaic of woods and heath

Animals and plants in focus

Grassland watch

40 The harvest mouse

46 The pygmy shrew

52 The little owl

58 The magpie

64 Spinners of silk

68 The harvestmen

70 Wild berries

75 Nightshades

78 Recognising grassland fungi

Woodland watch

84 Saving the common dormouse

88 Recognising bats

93 The goldcrest

99 The pheasant

105 Woodlice

107 Plant galls

111 Recognising woodland fungi

116 Three-pinnate ferns

121 Spurges and mercuries

126 Index

128 Acknowledgments

Introduction

Beaten down by rain, pitted by the hooves of grazing cattle and churned to a slew of sticky mud in gateways and around drinking troughs, an old overgrown pasture can be a sorry sight in autumn. The fresh green of early summer has long since faded and most of the flowers that brightened the grass have had their day. Yet its worn, battered look is deceptive. On closer inspection the damp soil is alive with small animals, and the plants that bore flowers in the summer are now bursting with seeds. Busy rooks and starlings strut and probe the soft ground, searching for worms and insect grubs. In a neglected corner, a flourishing crop of thistles attracts a twittering flock of goldfinches, perhaps fifty or more, intent on plucking the fluffy thistle seeds with their fine tweezer-like bills. At first they are surprisingly hard to see, their grey-brown backs blending with the vegetation, but when disturbed they burst up and dance through the air towards a nearby hedgerow, their yellow wingbars flashing in the autumn sun.

◄ Rooks welcome the cooler, wetter days of autumn that soften the soil and make probing for food easier. They often feed in large flocks, their glossy black plumage gleaming in the sun.

▲ Fallen fruit attracts worker wasps, which have little to do once their queens have stopped breeding. Soon they will be killed off by the frost, and only young mated queens survive.

▲ In autumn, the wild clematis that sprawls over hedgerows in chalk and limestone country becomes a mass of glinting, feathery fruits that explode into downy seed heads.

Hedgerow plenty

Goldfinches are not the only small birds that gather in flocks once the breeding season is over. In autumn, the hedges are full of linnets, greenfinches, chaffinches, yellowhammers and others that have banded together to forage for food. There is plenty for them to find. The hedges themselves glow with the haws and hips of hawthorn and wild rose, the plum-like sloes of blackthorn, the berries of bittersweet (see pages 75–77) and the feathery seed heads of traveller's joy. At the overgrown edges of fields, dense thickets of bramble are heavy with clusters of juicy blackberries – an irresistible feast for birds and insects alike (see pages 12–15 and 70–74). On nearby arable fields the stubble is surrounded by a scatter of spilt grain and wild-flower seeds, which are gleaned by bands of finches and buntings creeping over the ground like mice.

Butterflies, spiders and fungi

In early autumn some grassland flowers such as ragwort and tansy are still in bloom, providing nectar for bees and butterflies including the small copper and common blue. On the southern downs, late broods of clouded yellow butterflies hatch in September and October. Perhaps ten times a century huge numbers of these butterflies emerge, swarming over open grassland on sulphur-yellow wings. Clouded yellows are among the few butterflies that breed on cultivated crops, laying their eggs on the clovers and lucerne that are planted to increase the food value of silage and temporary pasture. Yet they cannot survive the cold, wet British winters. All the clouded yellows that appear in autumn are third generation immigrants, descended from those that arrived in spring from continental Europe. As the temperature falls in autumn they make their way towards the south coast and may even migrate back across the Channel. Observers on ships sailing well offshore have seen them heading south, flying low over the grey-green waves towards the distant shores of France.

▲ By mid-September the spiny blackthorns in hedgerows are covered with sloes. Despite their extremely sharp taste, they attract birds that eat them and spread their seed.

◄ Seeds and nuts scattered along the hedge bottom are gathered by bank voles. These blunt-faced, mouse-like rodents are the favourite prey of a host of hunters, from weasels to owls.

▶ October is the best month to watch the noisy displays of rutting red deer stags, which often festoon their magnificent antlers with vegetation torn from trees and bushes.

Many never make it and many more die before they get the chance to set off. Some are seized by flycatchers and other insect-eating birds to help fuel their own southward migrations, while others may fall prey to spiders that stretch their silken snares between the long grasses and hedgerows (see pages 64–67). On misty autumn mornings these webs are beaded with dew, which has the effect of extending each strand so the webs hang in loose, spangled loops. As the sun dries them, the strands shrink and tighten up, transforming the slack webs into taut, deadly traps.

Misty autumn mornings also provide the best opportunities to find grassland fungi (see pages 78–82). These include the field mushroom, the shaggy inkcap, the stately parasol mushroom and, most startling of all, the giant puffball, which can grow to a colossal 80cm (30in) across. Simply seeing them provides ample reward for an early walk through the dew-soaked grass.

Fungi spring up in woods, too, when the damp, yet still warm, weather gives their spores the best chance of germinating (see pages 111–115). They sprout overnight from rotting stumps and dead branches, or shoulder the leaf litter aside as they push up from the woodland floor. Some of these fungi are edible but many more are poisonous, for instance the colourful fly agaric that grows beneath birch trees and the sinister, aptly named death cap.

Falling leaves

All woodland fungi – with some exceptions, such as the parasitic honey fungus – feed on dead plant material and, along with woodlice (see pages 105–106) and other animals of the leaf litter, they play an important part in breaking down the millions of leaves that fall from the trees each autumn. The leaves are a symbol of the season – a kaleidoscopic array of yellow, brown, red and green carpeting the ground or still clinging to the branches. Some of the most spectacular colour is to be found in the beechwoods of southern and eastern England, where the green, gold and copper tones of the leaves form a glorious contrast with the silver-grey bark of the trees (see pages 20–23).

Magnificent timber trees such as oak rise high above low, multi-stemmed coppices of hazel, ash or chestnut. The bases of coppiced trees are often surprisingly broad. Originally cut to ground level every ten years or so in order to encourage new shoots for firewood, charcoal and fencing, these trees have never developed the tall trunks and spreading crowns of the uncoppiced timber trees that dwarf them. This

◄ As the late autumn frosts become more severe, grey squirrels spend less and less time in the open, and may have to defend favourite food resources against other squirrels.

▲ Like many birds, the nuthatch feeds heavily on nuts and seeds in autumn. It cracks open hazelnuts by wedging them in bark crevices, then attacking them with its bill.

▲ The curiously shaped leaves of the rare wild service tree can be seen only in ancient woodlands, where they turn gold and then crimson before falling to the ground.

periodic lopping has an advantage, however, because it has stopped them becoming top-heavy and prone to fatal collapse. They simply keep growing. Some coppiced trees are as much as 6m (20ft) across and some, at more than 1000 years old, are among the oldest living things in Britain.

Feeding flocks

Before they lose their leaves, deciduous trees develop the buds that will eventually burst into new foliage the following spring. The buds, and the tiny creatures that hide among them, provide food for small birds that forage through woodland in autumn. As on grassland they tend to roam in flocks, calling incessantly. They include the tiny goldcrest, the smallest of all British birds, the shrill calls of which are so high-pitched that many people cannot hear them at all (see pages 93–98). Goldcrests and long-tailed tits are agile, active and remarkably bold as they flit from tree to tree in feeding parties, in follow-my-leader fashion.

Many small birds, including coal tits, marsh tits and blue tits as well as goldcrests, move through the autumn woods in mixed-species flocks, partly because this improves their chances of finding good sources of food,

and partly because it provides some defence against predators such as sparrowhawks. Adapted for hunting among the trees, with relatively short wings and long tails for manoeuvrability, sparrowhawks are a deadly threat to small birds, especially where the foliage thins out and the birds are more exposed to attack. Feeding in a flock increases the number of vigilant eyes watching for danger and reduces the risk of any individual bird being picked off.

While small birds feed up in the branches, thrushes and jays pick through the leaves on the ground, searching for small animals, nuts and acorns. They are joined by squirrels, dormice (see pages 84–87) and other small mammals intent on eating – and in the case of jays and squirrels, storing – as much as possible before the coming winter. Autumn may sometimes seem like a fruitful extension of late summer, softened by mists and cushioned by colourful drifts of fallen leaves, but it is only a matter of time before the first frost sparkles on the hedgerow and winter sets in.

▲ Some moth caterpillars are still feeding in autumn. They include the spectacular larva of the pale tussock moth, which has defensive tufts of long bristles to deter hungry birds.

◄ Although most grassland flowers have faded, some gentians are at their best in autumn. They include the glorious fringed gentian, which grows only on the chalk grasslands of the Chilterns.

▲ Thanks to its acute hearing and silent flight, a hunting barn owl has no trouble pinpointing the faint rustling of a vole in the grass as it flies low over meadows and pastures.

Wildlife habitats and havens

- Bramble patches
- Ancient green lanes and tracks
- In and around an old beech tree
- The larch forest
- Woodland after dark
- The New Forest – mosaic of woods and heath

Bramble patches

Often impenetrable to larger creatures, brambles make ideal refuges for small animals and birds. They also provide food aplenty, especially in early autumn when their fruits ripen into sweet, juicy blackberries.

Many a track winding through meadows, fields and woods is lined with tangled thickets of bramble. One of the most widespread plants in Britain, the bramble is adaptable and vigorous enough to colonise such varied habitats as open pastures, woodland clearings, farm hedgerows, windswept clifftops, overgrown gardens and even derelict inner city sites. Despite the harsh treatment that it often receives, from mechanical hedge trimmers, for instance, the bramble is remarkably resilient. Indeed, it is quite difficult to kill, which makes it one of the most enduring features of the landscape.

Mature bramble thickets have an important ecological role to play in providing valuable places for a whole range of native wildlife to live, including insects, birds and small mammals. The jumbles of prickly stems are all but impenetrable to humans and other large mammals, so they provide safe havens for breeding birds. They also offer food in abundance for wildlife, especially later in the year when the berries are ripe and juicy. Many people enjoy the free harvest of wild berries, too, picking them for pies, jams and even wines.

Subtle differences
More than 400 distinct microspecies of bramble are found in the British Isles. Microspecies is the term used to describe closely related species that are biologically distinct but difficult to distinguish without using a

Brambles are often to be seen entwined in wayside scrub and hedgerows, their sinuous, prickly branches scrambling and weaving through the existing vegetation to create dense, thorny thickets.

DORMOUSE SHELTER

Brambles growing in open woodland clearings are very important to dormice. The flowers provide food in the form of pollen and nectar, and the nutritious fruits ripen soon after. Even the dried seeds will be eaten later in the year when other food supplies have dwindled.

Dormice spend most of their time in trees and shrubs, rarely visiting the ground, where they are vulnerable to predators such as stoats. When they do come down, however, bramble patches provide them with safe routes between the trees, reducing their need to expose themselves to danger.

Like many birds, dormice also make use of bramble patches as secure nesting sites. The matted stems provide an ideal base for constructing a safe nest woven from honeysuckle bark and soft leaves. The young are born in late summer, just as the bramble fruits ripen, so there is plenty of food for the suckling mother, and for the young dormice when they first venture from the nest.

Blackberries have a high sugar content and are an important source of energy for dormice as autumn approaches.

BRAMBLE FACT FILE

Brambles have many uses. As well as the berries providing food, the roots and fruits yield dye. Infusions of their leaves are used for herbal tea and as a traditional cure for sore throats, and have been used to treat wounds.

● NAMES
Common names: bramble, blackberry
Scientific name: *Rubus fruticosus* (agg.)

● HABITAT
Hedgerows and wayside scrub; fast-growing stems scramble effectively up almost anything; self-supporting bramble patches tend to grow outwards

● DISTRIBUTION
Throughout Britain and Ireland

● LEAVES
Compound, composed of 3–5 leaflets, each one oval with pointed tip, serrated edges and a thorny midrib underneath

● STEMS
Long and arching, woody at base, green to reddish brown, well endowed with sharp, slightly hooked thorns

● FLOWERS
Borne in clusters; each flower has 5 white, pink or mauve petals and produces copious nectar; appear May–September or even later

● FRUITS
Berries composed of many segments, each containing one seed; ripen from green to red to black; appear August–October

● USES
Berries are rich in vitamin C and also used along with leaves in traditional medicine, and for making dyes; stems used in wickerwork

The blackberries ripen sequentially throughout late summer and autumn, so the supply of fruit lasts several weeks or even months.

Blackberry clusters contain fruits at different stages of ripeness.

The bramble belongs to the rose family, and its delicate flowers are very similar to those of other wild roses such as dog rose and sweet briar.

Up to 5 leaflets make up the bramble leaf.

Sharp, curved thorns on the stems hook on to other plants.

hand lens or microscope. The word 'aggregate' (agg) after the scientific name indicates a microspecies. Brambles differ in small ways. Some flower at different times from others, for instance, and the fruits vary in size, texture and, most noticeably, flavour. This is why some bramble plants yield deliciously sweet, succulent blackberries, but others have small, gritty berries with a sharp or even a sour taste.

Shared features
Despite their variability, all microspecies of brambles share many characteristics. They have five-petalled flowers, indicating that they are part of the rose family, although the blooms can vary in colour from pure white to deep rose-pink or pale mauve. The flowers are prolific producers of nectar, which

attracts pollinating insects, such as bees and butterflies. After pollination the flowers give way to clusters of fruits, which are green and hard at first, but then turn red and finally purplish black when fully ripe. Each fruit is composed of many juicy segments, and inside each segment is a hard seed.

A bramble leaf is composed of three to five leaflets, each with a serrated margin, a pointed tip and a thorny midrib on the underside of the leaf. The leaf stalks are also thorny, as are the main stems. These stems are woody at the base when mature, but green and slightly angled on new growth.

Spiny colonists
Brambles are well adapted for colonising new areas. Long, arching stems grow out of the

main clump of a bramble patch. The spines on the stems enable them to cling to other vegetation, and scramble along hedgerows or climb up into the lower branches of overhanging trees. Alternatively, brambles may arch down to the ground, where they send out rootlets that anchor the plant and establish a secure base for its next advance into open space. In this way, fast-growing specimens can rapidly start to dominate the landscape.

They are particularly well suited to open, grassy areas, such as old, disused pasture, where the lack of regular grazing allows them to form dense thickets. Unable to flourish in the shade of mature trees, brambles usually occur in clearings or along open rides in woodlands. Nevertheless, they are useful

An adult speckled bush cricket feeds on the ripening fruit. These insects are usually killed by the first frosts of autumn.

in the early stages of tree growth – sapling trees can often get a good start by growing amid the thorny stems of brambles, which protect them from grazing deer and sheep. Eventually the trees grow through the

bramble canopy and develop to maturity, shading out the brambles that originally protected them.

Insect refuge
Many different types of insects live on brambles. Large colonies of aphids drink sap from the tender growing tips. Here they are preyed upon by ladybirds and their larvae, and by the voracious hoverfly larvae that visit the flowers to gather nectar.

Butterflies are regular visitors to brambles, and thickets growing in open areas often attract large numbers of gatekeeper butterflies in late summer. Late-flying species such as the comma and red admiral continue feeding on damaged, fermenting fruits well into autumn.

From late summer, bush crickets also become more noticeable. They sit out on sunny leaves during the day, but at night the rough rasping calls of the adult males may be heard coming from the base of the thicket. The females are silent, but they can be recognised by their ovipositors – the long tube at their rear – which they use

Wood mice nibble through the sweet, fleshy fruit segments to get at the hard seeds inside. These contain more nutritious food in the form of proteins essential for healthy growth.

to insert their eggs into the bases of the bramble stems. The eggs remain there for the winter and hatch in spring.

Bramble leaves are eaten by the caterpillars of various moths, such as the buff arches' moth. To avoid being eaten by birds, the caterpillars hide along twigs or under leaves during the day and emerge at night to feed. In autumn, they climb down the stems to the ground to pupate, emerging as adult moths the following summer.

Late autumn is a good time of year to look for the tunnels of the bramble leaf miner, a tiny moth caterpillar that lives inside the leaf, feeding on the tissues from within. The strange contorted growths on the stems caused by bramble gall wasps can also be more easily seen as the leaves fall away late in the year.

Feeding birds
The abundance of insects attracts insect-eating birds such as the whitethroat, which finds both plentiful food and safe nesting sites in bramble patches. Its soft, churring call can be heard well into early autumn, when the ripe blackberries provide valuable

Roe deer often feed on bramble foliage. It can be a vital source of food in late autumn, when the leaves of many other shrubs have withered and fallen.

RELATED SPECIES

Found throughout much of Britain, the dewberry is a relative of the bramble but has weaker, rounded stems with fewer prickles. It is a much smaller plant and the flowers are always white. Although the fruits are smaller with fewer segments, each segment is larger with a whitish, waxy-looking bloom.

Cloudberry, which is confined to upland areas, is even smaller than dewberry. It has rounded, lobed leaves and solitary white flowers. Stone bramble, which is smaller still, normally grows in shady, rocky places. It has spineless stems and pure white flowers, and its leaves always have three leaflets.

▲ **Stone bramble is found in the kind of rocky woodland associated with hill country, and its rather poor berries seem to reflect these harsh conditions.**

▶ **Identifiable by the pale, waxy bloom on its fruits, dewberry is widespread on rough grassland and sand dunes, especially in eastern Britain, but does not occur in northern Scotland.**

extra food as the bird builds up its reserves, ready for its long flight to Africa.

While the whitethroat flies south in autumn, many other small birds stay behind. These include the secretive dunnock, which can be hard to see as it feeds in the shade beneath bramble patches, shuffling over the ground like a mouse, foraging for insects and seeds. Even more elusive than the

dunnock is the wren, which feeds in the deep cover of bramble patches. Earlier in the year both species use the thorny thickets as secure nesting sites, and sometimes a discarded container or an old boot tossed into the brambles will provide a nesting box for a pair of wrens.

The long-tailed tit has no interest in such ready-made refuges, but it often builds its

▲ **The long-tailed tit nests in bramble patches on commons and in the clearings and fringes of woodland. The snarled thorny stems offer welcome security.**

exquisite domed nest in a bramble patch. When the leaves thin out in autumn these nests become more visible, revealing the intricacy of their construction. The outer layers are built up of mosses and lichens, bound together with sticky threads of cobweb to create a soft pouch, lined with downy feathers and soft mammal hair. The patchwork of moss and lichen provides excellent camouflage within the shady brambles.

Autumn larder

The blackberries start to appear on the brambles in late summer and persist throughout the autumn. The fruit provides valuable food for birds and mammals as these creatures build up their weight ready for the coming

winter, or to fuel long migration flights. As they feed, the mammals and birds spread the bramble seeds, which pass unharmed through their digestive systems and are eventually scattered in their droppings.

When the weather gets colder, the bramble patch enters a quieter period. The fruits have been eaten and the insect population has all but disappeared, but the brambles are still sought out by some animals. The leaves that persist on the stems are often the only green vegetation available to deer and rabbits at this time, and since even the hardest frost will not damage them, they can be a valuable source of winter food.

As the leaves are gradually stripped away, the importance of bramble patches as nesting sites and refuges becomes more obvious. Old birds' nests can be seen perched among the twisting stems. Tiny grassy cups low down in the bush are usually the nests of warblers, while larger mud-lined cups are the remains of nests built by song thrushes. The shelter that brambles provide for

rabbits is also very apparent in winter, as their runways and burrow entrances show up far more clearly when most of the stems are bare.

A heavy fall of winter snow will sometimes cover a bramble patch, but its network of tangled stems provides enough support to leave a clear area beneath, sheltered from the cold winds. This provides a welcome retreat for small birds such as wrens, robins and dunnocks, as well as voles, mice and sometimes predatory stoats.

The dunnock usually feeds on the ground, and often finds plenty to eat beneath the dense cover of a flourishing bramble thicket.

▼ **Bramble often grows in hedgerows and along waysides entwined with other hardy plants, such as holly and honeysuckle, that share its rambling habit.**

Ancient green lanes and tracks

The half-forgotten grassy lanes that thread between meadows and fields are relics of a bygone age. Some still provide shelter for plants and animals that have lived there for centuries.

A close look at a detailed map of almost any country parish will soon reveal a network of tracks and byways extending like a spider's web across the landscape. These rustic lanes follow the lie of the land, unlike most recently planned roads, curving with the contours and conforming to the pattern of fields and woods.

In medieval times all lanes were 'green'. Even major routes between cities were little more than rutted tracks. As motor vehicles came into general use, hard road surfacing became almost universal for public roads, yet some lanes never carried enough traffic to justify the expense. Ignored by road authorities, and often partly overgrown, these ancient routeways survive as grassy green lanes or tracks.

Lanes differ from tracks by virtue of their boundaries rather than the route they take. Essentially, green lanes include all unmetalled tracks that are bounded by hedges, ditches or walls. Any byways that are not confined in this way are called tracks.

Routes through history

Where lanes and tracks are still used by farm vehicles they are likely to be brown rather than green – earth rather than grass. Nevertheless, they are nearly always ancient in origin. The oldest of these byways, such as the ridgeways over the chalk downs, can be traced back to prehistoric times, although Roman, Saxon and medieval travellers all contributed to the track network at later dates. The routes were used by pilgrims, cattle drovers, itinerant tradesmen and farmers, as well as packhorses and carts carrying produce ranging from stone and timber to salt, pottery, glassware and trinkets.

Wild diversity

Today the routes carry little traffic, if any, and they are usually isolated from the destructive effects of modern farming. As a result, their grass verges, ditches and hedgebanks are often among the wildest places in the locality, and have been so for centuries. This long-term stability is excellent for wildlife because various plants and the animals associated with them have had time to evolve relatively undisturbed.

The animal life supported by these quiet byways is often evident from signs of activity among the taller vegetation.

The barn owl may be on the wing in the late afternoon as well as at night in autumn. Quiet country pathways offer abundant prey and safe hunting.

▼ Honeysuckle is a sturdy plant that pervades many waysides, its woody stems entwining any convenient trees and shrubs. It flowers from June to September, when bright red berries appear, each one containing several seeds.

Hawthorn thrives alongside many country tracks. Its rich red berries are relished by many birds and hoarded by small mammals, such as bank voles, stock-piling for winter.

WEB OF LIFE

On any country track the plants and animals form a complex interconnected food chain, so no one species lives in isolation. On the green lanes of west Oxfordshire, for example, the rare downy woundwort plays a role in the lives of many animals. Rabbits and deer graze the whole plant, and at least one species of caterpillar mines the leaves and stems. In autumn its ripe seeds are eaten by wood mice, voles and finches. The seeds are heavy and rarely dispersed far, so the plant does not spread easily. It relies on some disturbance of the ground to get established and suppress competing plants. Green lanes with sparse yet regular traffic are ideal places.

▼ The bank vole's varied diet of fruit, leaves and flowers enables it to flourish in many trackside areas, where it is active during the day.

▲ A type of dead-nettle, downy woundwort is confined to a few green lanes and verges in the Wychwood Forest region of Oxfordshire.

Tunnels through the grass, worn tracks, trampled leaves and bent stems mark the passage of scores of small mammals. Wood mice and bank voles frequent the grass verges, emerging from the shelter of hedgerows to feed on flowers, seeds and new shoots. They take a substantial risk in doing so, since sharp-eyed kestrels often hover above the lanes watching for prey, or launch deadly ambushes from vantage points on fences, trees and overhead wires. At night barn owls patrol the broader grassy verges on silent wings, listening for the faint rustle and squeak that may indicate the presence of prey.

Long grass on trackside verges may be frequented by the harvest mouse. The traditional image of this diminutive rodent shows it weaving its intricate nest among gently swaying stems of wheat, but in these days of combine harvesters the mouse is far more likely to breed in rough grass around field boundaries. Harvest mice breed well into early autumn, and their spherical nests of woven grass stems, about the size of tennis balls, can often be found on the margins of green lanes.

Mammals and birds

Where byways wind uphill, often skirting ancient woods and ponds, they may be flanked by sunny banks and rocky outcrops, and offer spectacular views of the surrounding landscape. Since the routes are not regularly used by humans,

HOLLOW WAYS

Sunken lanes that cut deeply through banks were once known as hollow ways. They often skirt the edges of woodland, where they were probably used for carting firewood and timber. Some hollow ways run through natural ravines, but most of them have gradually deepened with use. Their unmetalled surfaces have been eroded

◄ **The distinctive hart's-tongue fern grows in circular clumps on banks, its tropical-looking leaves unfurling as they grow out from the centre.**

► An age-old favourite, the primrose has been brightening the steep banks of lanes and hollow ways for centuries. In days gone by they were renowned for a variety of medicinal and supposedly magical properties.

over the centuries, not so much by passing feet and wheels, but by sudden storms turning them into temporary channels for torrents of rainwater.

Some really deep hollow ways run under the boles and roots of trees, and form dark, damp, earthy, fern-lined tunnels. Others are flanked by steep banks that, thanks to shelter from scorching sun and withering wind, support a colourful succession of wild flowers from spring to autumn.

Such places often have a primeval, almost magical air, due in part to the abundance of primitive plants including mosses, liverworts and ferns such as the hart's-tongue, with its glossy, strap-shaped fronds. Flowers include the Cornish moneywort, which is found only in damp, shady places. It has tiny, long-stalked whitish flowers and a sprawl of circular leaves, each the size of a medieval silver halfpenny.

they offer the chance to see animals that shy away from busier thoroughfares. From the shelter of a hedge or wall dividing crop fields it is often possible to watch brown hares, especially after the crops have been harvested. Other creatures, such as rabbits, deer and badgers, are most active at dawn and dusk, and at these times it may also be possible to watch a hungry fox stalk and catch its prey.

For these animals, the lanes and tracks provide convenient routes to feeding areas. Unlike the treacherous ribbons of tarmac that dominate so much of the modern landscape, these old pathways present the animals with little risk of being run down and killed. Even when they do carry traffic, the vehicles usually move slowly enough for the animals to avoid them.

After rain, the ruts and dips are usually muddy, and are ideal places to look for the tracks of animals that may have passed by. In areas with clay soil, the churned-up earth around gates and stiles provides perfect

building material for birds that line or build their nests with mud. House martins, for instance, which often breed under the eaves of nearby buildings, mould their nests entirely from mud and clay, and the swallows that nest inside farm buildings use a mixture of mud and dry grass.

Swallows and martins do well to nest in the vicinity of green lanes because during the warmer months the sheltered air of lanes flanked by tall

▼ A brown hare is easy to see on bare or recently sown fields in autumn. The hare leaves characteristic runs and marks in the long grass that usually lines green lanes.

▲ The large flat flower-heads of yarrow attract the nectar-feeding small copper butterfly, which can be seen on the wing well into October.

◄ The tiny harvest mouse raises a litter of three to seven babies in a nest carefully woven of grass and plant stems.

banks or hedgerows often swarms with insects seeking nectar from wayside plants. They provide a bonanza for insect-eating birds well into September. As the sun sinks below the horizon, the birds may be joined, and eventually supplanted, by bats, especially if there is water nearby – which is often the case as lanes are commonly edged by ditches. Guided by their highly developed sonar, these nimble aerial hunters dart and jink through the gloom, flickering silhouettes against the darkening sky.

Plants and insects

Many wild flowers and shrubs are so tied to ancient green lanes that they can be treated as evidence of the land's antiquity. The rare and beautiful meadow clary is such a plant. It lives on the limestone of Oxfordshire and a few similar chalk downlands, but without old tracks it would have difficulty surviving because, while this plant favours old lime-rich grassland, it cannot tolerate the intensive grazing of sheep and rabbits that is typical of this habitat.

▼ While crops are harvested mechanically, small animals find refuge in the vegetation that lines the chalk trackways of the South Downs. Such wild fringes are vital to the survival of farmland wildlife.

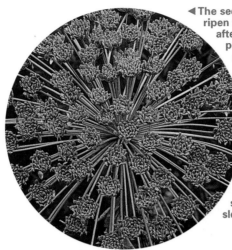

◀ The seed heads of hogweed ripen from September, after they have been pollinated by an army of insects. The roots of hogweed were once harvested as pig fodder.

▶ The spiny teasel often grows in abundance alongside green lanes and tracks. In autumn and winter the seeds are an important source of food for the slender-billed goldfinch.

The verges of green lanes are often enriched by animal dung and soil washed off the track surface by rain, and so typically they support tall, lush vegetation such as umbellifers, thistles, docks, hedge garlic and, in chalky districts, knapweed and meadow crane's-bill. Although limited in the variety of species they support, such verges are a rich source of nectar and pollen for insects, and in autumn they provide plenty of ripe fruits and seeds for birds.

On still, warm days in early autumn the flowers of ragwort or hogweed are often still alive with hoverflies, craneflies, soldier beetles, weevils and, in the case of ragwort, the odd darting small copper butterfly. The hogweed's strong smell of pig is a reminder that wild flower scents are not for

human benefit. To a fly or beetle, the scent of hogweed is irresistible, and while the insects feed they are carrying pollen from bloom to bloom.

Without green lanes and their unmanaged grassy verges, overgrown hedgerows and flooded ditches, many such plants might become scarce. So, of course, would the insects, nesting birds and small mammals that depend on them. A walk down a grassy lane or track reveals just part of the complex web of life

that it supports – a dragonfly hawking for midges, a twittering gang of goldfinches raiding thistle heads for seeds, or a hunting weasel streaking across a path. They all rely on a habitat that has evolved over centuries and miraculously survived into the modern world.

In and around an old beech tree

A carpet of fallen leaves encourages rare plants to take root, while hollows in the trunk provide shelter for birds, squirrels, mice and bats.

The beech is a native tree that colonised the south-eastern corner of Britain at least 8000 years ago, after the last Ice Age ended but before Britain became an island. It spread north and west across eastern and southern England, and is now one of the commonest woodland trees on the chalk hills of the south.

Beeches have also been deliberately planted in parks and open areas of grassland, and these plantings often take the form of avenues and hilltop groves. They include landmarks such as Wittenham Clumps near Wallingford in Oxfordshire and Chanctonbury Ring on the South Downs in Sussex, which was largely destroyed by the great storm of 1987 but has since been replanted. Both of these sites are ancient hillforts and are visible for miles.

Beech trees grow best in relatively light, free-draining soils. They are most abundant in chalk country, but they will grow in acid soils provided their roots do not become waterlogged. In fact, they seem able to tolerate the worst of the British climate and some of the most impoverished soils, having been introduced in the far north and west, well beyond their natural, self-sown range. However, these northern specimens usually have shorter trunks and a less stately form than southern trees.

Room to grow
Beech trees naturally grow in close proximity to each other, forming dense woodland. The crowding tends to produce rather thin-trunked trees and the most magnificent beeches grow in managed woodlands and parks, where the trees are regularly thinned out to allow the survivors ample room to spread and grow. Their smooth, cylindrical trunks may be 3m (10ft) across at the base, and rise sheer for 20m (65ft) before branching. Such trees can attain heights of up to 40m (130ft), with sturdy domed profiles.

Beech woods with a long history of management often contain trees that once were pollarded. This means that the trees were regularly cut down to a height of 2–3m (7–10ft). The stumps sprouted a regular crop of new growth safely beyond the reach of hungry deer and ponies. Beech trees were pollarded in order to produce crops of slender poles and most of these pollards were last cut well over a century ago. Their trunks now bear large bosses and massive, often contorted branches.

Shade-loving plants
Young beech saplings can tolerate the deep shade caused by any mature trees growing close together, but as they reach maturity themselves, they tend to shade out other species, and eventually only the beeches remain.

The lack of light limits the variety of plants that can grow beneath the trees, and the floor of a beech wood often appears to be little more than a carpet of fallen leaves. These are gradually broken down by fungi, which – unlike green plants – do not require light to grow.

In the south of England, beech trees can reach gigantic proportions. Grown for their very hard, fine-grained timber, such trees were deliberately thinned out to give them space to grow as big as possible.

BEECH FACT FILE

The elegant form, smooth silvery bark and glorious leaf colour of the beech in spring and autumn make it easy to identify. The species is native to Britain south of a line from the Bristol Channel to the Wash. North of this line it grows as a result of deliberate introductions.

The fruits of beech develop inside spiky cases, which split open when ripe to release two triangular seeds.

● **NAME**
Common name: beech
Scientific name: *Fagus sylvatica*

● **HABITAT**
Mainly dry, light soils

● **DISTRIBUTION**
Throughout Britain, but most common in the south

● **HEIGHT**
Up to 40m (130ft)

● **LIFESPAN**
Up to 250 years

● **BARK**
Smooth silver-grey

● **LEAVES**
Shiny green above and below, with a wavy margin and prominent veins; yellow, then orange-brown in autumn before falling, but on very young trees they remain attached all winter

● **TRUNK AND BRANCHES**
Mature trees have massive, cylindrical trunks, with uplifted branches

● **BUDS**
Slender and pointed, with smooth brown scales

● **FLOWERS**
Separate male and female flowers are produced in early summer; male flowers are greenish yellow and hang down on short stalks; female flowers are reddish and encased in small green cups on very short stalks

● **FRUITS**
Known as beech mast; two triangular, shiny brown seeds encased in a prickly four-valved husk

● **USES**
An attractive ornamental tree; timber excellent for making furniture and kitchen utensils, but of little use outside because it is prone to rapid decay

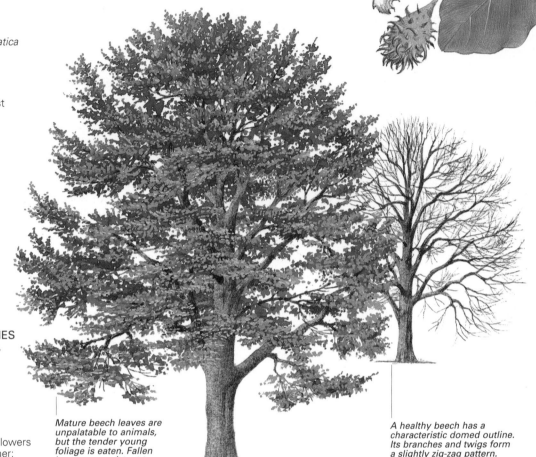

Mature beech leaves are unpalatable to animals, but the tender young foliage is eaten. Fallen leaves are resistant to decay and take a long time to rot.

A healthy beech has a characteristic domed outline. Its branches and twigs form a slightly zig-zag pattern.

BEECH MAST

In a good year, beech trees produce vast crops of seeds known as beech mast. The seeds are very attractive to birds and mammals, and most of the crop is either eaten or stored for the winter. Many common woodland birds, such as great tits, nuthatches and chaffinches, congregate to feast on a good crop of mast. Grey squirrels gorge themselves, hoarding what they can't eat immediately. Dormice, which also nest in beech trees, take advantage of the plentiful food supply to fatten up before their long winter hibernation.

► **Beech mast provides many animals with nutrient-rich food in autumn, giving them a better chance of surviving the winter ahead.**

▶ Birds that nest in holes in beech trees include the nuthatch. Nuthatches plaster mud over the cavity entrances to keep out predators and egg thieves.

▼ The rare and mysterious ghost orchid survives without the green pigment used by other plants to convert sunlight into energy.

Bramblings come to Britain in the autumn, when they can often be seen pecking at beech mast alongside other finches.

The bare ground provides ideal conditions for mosses, such as the white fork moss, which forms compact, pale greyish green cushions on old tree stumps as well as on the ground. Each cushion contains many individual plants, and the cushions often join up to form an undulating green carpet.

On chalky soils the hart's-tongue fern may grow beneath beech trees. The fern's bright-green, undivided fronds were given their name long ago because of their supposed resemblance to the tongue of the hart, or male fallow deer. Orange lines on the underside of the mature fronds are rows of sori, the structures that produce the plant's reproductive spores in autumn and winter. A spore must land somewhere damp in order to develop into a small, flattened, heart-shaped structure called a gametophyte. If the conditions are right, this produces male and female cells that fuse to produce new ferns.

Pallid ghosts

One of the most elusive beechwood plants is the ghost orchid. The gloom of the woodland floor suits it because the plant does not need light to make food. It has no green parts at all and relies on a fungus to provide it with nutrients. Its strange, semi-transparent flower spikes may push through the leaf litter at any time from May to October. There are no leaves, just a waxy-looking stem and flowers, which have a sickly smell and are often eaten by slugs before they get the chance to set seed. Perhaps not surprisingly, the ghost orchid has always been extremely rare. It has been seen just a few times in recent years, and only in the beechwoods of the south Chilterns. Now, it may even be extinct in Britain.

Rather more robust, and seen far more regularly, is the bird's-nest orchid, another species that lacks green leaves and depends on a fungus to provide it with nutrients. Its name derives from the curious arrangement of its roots, which look rather like an untidy bird's nest. A similar

The carpet of dead beech leaves below the trees provides an ideal damp habitat for drought-sensitive molluscs, including the tiny cheese snail.

plant, the yellow bird's nest, which belongs to the family Monotropaceae, also grows in shady beech woodlands, where it feeds on dead and decaying matter. Its scale-like leaves are yellow at first but turn honey brown in autumn, making it very difficult to spot on the woodland floor.

Unpalatable leaves

Organisms that usually cause decay find the fallen leaves of beeches difficult to break down, so dead leaves often lie in deep layers beneath the trees. While they are still growing on the tree, the leaves are equally unpalatable to most invertebrates, but a few caterpillars eat them. These include the lobster moth caterpillar, which feeds on the leaves in summer.

When it first hatches from the egg, this curious insect looks rather like a small ant, and as it grows larger it develops strange outgrowths that give it a bizarre lobster-like appearance. By September it has finished feeding and climbs down into the leaf litter. Here it forms a pupa inside a silken cocoon, where it remains until the following summer and then emerges as an adult moth.

The leaf litter shelters other insects, too, such as the wood cricket. Active by day and night, the wood cricket forages among the debris for small animals, which it chews up in its strong jaws.

The damp leaves are home to slugs and snails, which are able to digest woody plant fibre, helping to recycle materials that other organisms cannot use. Many of them feed on rotting plant material, while others attack fungi, including species that are extremely poisonous to people. The slugs include the small and rather attractive lemon slug, which has a pure yellow body with dark tentacles. The lemon slug is often to be found on fungi in autumn, especially after heavy rain.

The much larger, ashy grey slug also eats fungi, but usually stays out of sight beneath the leaf litter. The tiny cheese snail is even harder to find, being restricted to a few old beechwoods in the south of England. Its flattened shape resembles a whole cheese, and when young its shell appears slightly hairy.

Death and decay

The natural life span of a beech is around 250 years. However, beeches growing in shallow soils are vulnerable to gale-force winds and may be blown down long before they reach this age. The roots form a shallow plate that spreads

Hart's-tongue ferns grow on calcareous soils, in the damp leaf litter found under beech trees.

BEECH TREE FUNGI

The porcelain fungus *Oudemansiella mucida* is a common sight on old beech trees, glistening in the autumn sunlight as it grows in small clusters out of the trunk or main branches. This fungus is ivory white and always covered with a thin slimy coating. Its appearance signals that the tree is under attack, as the fruiting bodies of the fungus are only part of the organism. The mycelium, or main body of the fungus, grows deep inside the trunk of the tree, feeding on any dead tissues.

One of Britain's most poisonous fungi, the death cap *Amanita phalloides*, may be found growing beneath old beech trees. The cap is rounded at first and then flat when fully open. It is a greenish olive colour with a slight shine, and it may have a slightly streaked appearance caused by thin radiating fibres on the top. All other parts of the fungus are white with a faint greenish or yellowish flush, and the stem

sits in a white basal bulb. The death cap is well named because it is lethally poisonous and accounts for several fatalities each year through liver and kidney failure. Despite this, the cap sometimes shows signs of feeding slugs, which may be unaffected by the poison.

The beechwood sickener, or *Russula nobilis*, is an attractive fungus with a flattened red cap and a brittle white stem. The rest of the fungus is pure white, and the flesh has a peculiar smell of coconut. This species can be one of the commonest toadstools in a beechwood in autumn, enlivening the rather bare woodland floor with its bright red caps. It, too, is poisonous, and should not be eaten, despite its attraction to woodland creatures.

Distinctive fungi, such as this poisonous *Russula*, grow in the leaf litter below beech trees in autumn.

laterally like a disc, but does not extend very deeply into the ground. The roots may support the tree for many decades, but fail in a high wind. Whole beechwoods growing on shallow chalk soils in the south-east were toppled by the severe storm of 1987.

Even a well-established tree growing in deep soil will eventually succumb to the attacks of fungi and die. This can happen very quickly. An apparently healthy tree may lose all its leaves and sprout a crop of fungi, sometimes within a few months. In fact, fungi live in the tree all the time, in small areas of damaged wood, and start to thrive when the living tree loses its vigour.

Fungi are not the only organisms ready to take advantage of a dying tree. When branches fall off, they leave scars which, with a little

work, form ideal nesting sites for woodpeckers and nuthatches. Deeper cavities in the trunk are exploited by owls, jackdaws and stock doves. Squirrels and dormice may also move into these deep hollows, and bats may use them as daytime roosts.

All these refuges are temporary because a dead beech rarely remains standing for long. Weakened by decay, it will eventually crash to the ground, providing food for timber-boring insects and more fungi. By degrees the process of decay destroys the timber, returning its nutrients to the soil where they can be taken up by young beech seedlings sprouting from the carpet of fallen leaves.

WILDLIFE WATCH

Where can I see beechwoods?

● Beeches are abundant on the chalk hills of the North and South Downs and Chilterns, and the limestone Cotswolds.

● Burnham Beeches near Slough and parts of Windsor Great Park have splendid beechwoods.

● Beeches grow well on the old red sandstone around Cardiff and in parts of Powys.

● Symonds Yat, on the River Wye in the forest of Dean, is surrounded by impressive beechwoods. The trees are well suited to the local limestone soils.

● Epping Forest, to the north of London, and Blean Woods near Canterbury both contain tracts of beechwood, which grow among other mixed deciduous trees.

The larch forest

Among the most graceful of conifers, larches grow in light and airy plantations that are home to colourful fungi and unusual birds.

Few of the trees that commonly grow in the woodlands of Britain are as distinctive as larches. Unusually for cone-bearing conifer trees, larches are deciduous and lose their needle-shaped leaves in autumn. So, unlike most conifers, which are evergreen, their appearance is constantly changing, from the bare branches of winter to the fresh green foliage of spring and the glowing yellow of autumn. The trees themselves have an airy grace that most evergreen conifers lack, with elegant downswept branches that curve up at the ends.

There are no native species of larch. All those that are growing in Britain have been planted, mostly as commercial timber crops. Such plantations are never as rich in wildlife as native woodland, because exotic trees are of limited value to wild plants and animals that have evolved to live on and among native species. Larch plantations are richer in wildlife than most, however. The lack of thick foliage in spring allows a wide variety of plants to grow beneath the trees and, in autumn, the larches' cones attract seed-eating birds. A number of different fungi may also be found at this time, pushing their way through the debris on the plantation floor.

Most larch plantations are of European larch, an elegant, upright species that comes from the Alps and Carpathian mountains. It was first brought to Britain around 380 years ago for its decorative qualities, to grace the grounds of stately homes. However, the larch's practical attributes soon became apparent and it was recognised as an important commercial tree.

By as long ago as the late 18th century, a vast acreage of larch woodland had already been established.

Floral highlights

Larch plantations can be surprisingly rewarding for plant-lovers prepared to do a little careful searching. Margins and open rides tend to be the most productive areas, partly because they are much sunnier than the shady interior, which promotes plant growth.

The trees themselves have a direct influence on the ground conditions, and therefore on the flowers that will grow. As with other conifers, their needles are resinous and slow to decay. Layer upon layer build up over the years and in dense plantations the effect on low-growing plants may be so stifling that almost nothing survives. Where the trees are more generously spaced, the ground flora often flourishes.

▶ In autumn, larch needles turn spectacular shades of yellow and gold before they fall, contributing a marvellous spectacle to the countryside.

◀ Although its bill is not adapted for the job, the goldfinch is often able to extract seeds from over-mature larch cones. These birds also forage for insects.

▲ The rufous milkcap is one of several species of fungi to be found sprouting in larch woods in autumn.

EUROPEAN LARCH FACT FILE

The European larch is a tall, distinctive conifer, which grows relatively fast but seldom lives very long. Unlike native British conifers, it is deciduous.

● **NAMES**
Common name: European larch, Common larch
Scientific name: *Larix decidua*

● **HABITAT**
Most soil types

● **DISTRIBUTION**
Planted commercially throughout Britain in both lowlands and uplands

● **HEIGHT**
Up to 45m (150ft)

● **LIFESPAN**
Usually 30–40 years

● **BARK**
Varies in colour from pale brown to grey; thickest at base of trunk

● **NEEDLES**
20–30mm (¾–1¼in) long, pale green in spring, turn golden yellow in autumn; borne in tufts of 30–40

● **BRANCHES**
Knotted, yellowish and pendulous

● **FLOWERS**
Small, cone-like; whitish then yellowish in male and pink then reddish in female; appear March–April; female flowers enlarge and darken into cones as they mature

● **SEEDS**
Borne in cones, 20–30mm (¾–1¼in) long, comprising 40–50 scales; ripen in autumn; mature cones remain on tree for several years after seeds have been shed

● **USES**
Varied including fence posts, boat building and pulp for paper production

Branches radiate horizontally from the trunk in irregular whorls.

Sweeping, pendulous branches and twigs.

Pale green needles are borne in tufts.

A mature cone is brown and woody.

A broad base supports a straight, upright trunk.

The mature female flowers of the European larch are reddish and cone-shaped with tightly packed scales. When fertilised they ripen into the brown, woody cones that contain the tree's seeds.

JAPANESE LARCH

The Japanese larch, *Larix kaempferi*, is widely grown in Britain. It is especially common on the poor soils of upland and western regions, where it grows better than its European counterpart. It is also more resistant to fungal disease. In fact, the Japanese larch is more widespread and numerous in plantations around the world than it is in its native habitat, on the slopes of Mount Fuji in Japan.

Superficially similar to the European larch in growth habits and form, the Japanese larch can be recognised by the blue-green hue of its needles, which have two pale grey bands on their lower surface. To complicate matters, however, a hybrid larch, *Larix x eurolepis*, derived from Japanese and European parents is also widely planted in Britain. It displays characteristics of both species and has the 'hybrid vigour' that is typical of such crosses.

Introduced in 1861, the Japanese larch thrives in the wetter western half of Britain. The deciduous needles are clustered in rosettes, like those of the European larch.

▼ The common crossbill benefits from larch plantations, since the cones' seeds provide food in winter when other seeds are scarce.

► Larch needles fall off each autumn, but the mature, seed-bearing cones persist on the twigs for several years.

Larches are surprisingly tolerant of soil type and are grown in a wide range of settings, from chalk downland to moorland slopes and free-draining, acid sand or gravel. The range of plants to be found beneath the canopy of a larch wood reflects the soil and location of the area, so is likely to be broadly similar to the flora of nearby deciduous woodland and hedgerows.

In lowland Britain, ground-layer plants often include species such as bramble, greater stitchwort and perhaps lesser celandine. Carpets of bluebells grow on a number of sites with chalk or neutral soils, often alongside wood spurge, wood anemone and dog's mercury, creating a wonderful tapestry of colour in spring. By contrast, in larch woods on acid soils the ground vegetation tends to resemble that of moors and heaths, and is dominated by plants such as ling – a type of heather – and bilberry.

Fruitful fungi

If spring is the time to watch for woodland flowers, autumn is the season for tracking down fungi. Larch woods are unusually rich in these strange, ephemeral organisms – from early September to late November a succession of toadstools and other fungal fruiting bodies force their way through the mass of larch needles on the woodland floor, or burst from decaying tree stumps.

Among those that shed their spores through pores beneath their caps instead of gills, the larch bolete, *Suillus grevillei*, with its orange tan cap, is one of the most characteristic fungi of larch forests. Indeed, it seems to be unable to survive in the absence of larch trees. Several other *Suillus* species are also common, *S. viscidus* for example, as are closely related members of the genus *Boletus*, including the bay bolete, *Boletus badius*.

Many of the fungi found in larch woods are of the gilled variety. The latex-exuding rufous milkcap, *Lactarius rufus*, is a familiar sight along with several other members of the *Lactarius* group. Another common species is the plums-and-custard fungus,

INSECT LIFE

Although densely planted larch woodland can seem devoid of insect life, mature forests with open sunny rides harbour a whole range of species. For example, a larch plantation in southern England is likely to provide a home for the scorpionfly, which feeds on dead insects and fruit, and butterflies such as the speckled wood and gatekeeper, which gather nectar from woodland floor flowers and brambles. In upland districts, however, horse flies and hoverflies are probably more common.

These are all found in various other habitats too, but larch trees do support a few more specialised insects. Easily overlooked because of their small size, some aphid relatives called adelgids often occur in huge numbers during the warmer months. In particular, *Adelgis abietis* – sometimes called the pseudocone gall aphid – is the favourite food of the larch ladybird, *Aphidecta obliterata*.

▲ Although the scorpionfly does not depend directly on larch trees for food, it often occurs in open rides through larch plantations.

► The larch ladybird preys upon the aphids that feed on larches and may spend most of its life on its namesake tree.

▲ Despite its small size – up to 10cm (4in) – the vivid colour of the yellow antler fungus makes it conspicuous when it sprouts from the forest floor.

▲ The little coal tit is a year-round resident in many larch woods, where it searches the foliage for insects, including aphids and caterpillars.

Tricholomopsis rutilans, which owes its delightful name to its red and yellow cap. Among the most intriguing in appearance are the earth-fan, *Thelephora terrestris*, and the yellow antler fungus, *Calocera viscosa*. Both grow on wood that is partly buried in the soil.

Foraging birds

Larch forests do not harbour as much variety in birdlife as native deciduous woods, but some of the species to be seen feeding among the trees are real conifer specialists. They include the coal tit, which seems to find larch forests much to its liking, and may even breed in them when the trees are mature enough for holes to form in their trunks. The tiny goldcrest can also be seen foraging acrobatically among the foliage, its presence betrayed by its extremely high, thin calls.

Both these birds may also feed in deciduous woodland, but the common crossbill is found only among larch and other conifer trees. Its cross-tipped mandibles are an adaptation for extracting seeds from cones and the birds eat very little else. The seeds of European and Japanese larches are important in their diet because the cones of both trees ripen in autumn and yield seeds right through the winter, a time when food is otherwise scarce. In the absence of larches, it is doubtful whether crossbill populations could flourish in Britain. As it is, the birds are often forced to scatter widely in search of new food sources.

Another species associated with conifer trees is the long-eared owl. These owls often nest among larches, and although they are strictly nocturnal, a visit at dusk may be rewarded by a glimpse of an owl's ghostly shape flying over a ride.

The woodcock is also active at dusk, although it is even more elusive than the long-eared owl. If a woodcock is disturbed at its resting place among the fallen needles on the forest floor, it will fly up on broad wings and zigzag away into the dark.

▲ A sunny, grassy clearing in a larch wood may be adopted by the speckled wood butterfly as its territory. Late broods are to be seen until mid-October.

WILDLIFE WATCH

Where can I see larch forests?

● Larch plantations can be found in most parts of Britain except the far west.

● There are plenty of mature larch forests in the Chiltern Hills in the south of England, where the trees were planted in an attempt to harmonise plantations of alien evergreen conifers with native woodland.

● In the New Forest, mature larches are a favourite haunt of crossbills in winter. The bigger trees are used for nesting by numerous birds of prey, including scarce goshawks.

● Several plantations of Japanese larch are to be found in Snowdonia National Park.

● European larch has been used to create shelter belts and small woodlands in the Lake District. Japanese larch is often used for more extensive planting.

● Large tracts of mature larches can be found in Northumberland National Park and Kielder Forest.

● Larch plantations occur throughout the Peak District National Park, but the best examples of mature trees can be found near Ladybower Reservoir and in the Derwent Valley.

◄ The woodcock is a wader but prefers to live in damp woodland, including larch forests, rather than marshes.

Woodland after dark

As dusk falls, disconcerting rustles and squeaks of small nocturnal animals may be heard in the undergrowth, while overhead the hoots of hunting owls echo eerily through the trees.

Nightfall in woodland has a timeless quality that, for the nervous, can be uncomfortably evocative of spine-chilling tales of witches and wild beasts. The reassuring twitterings of small woodland birds slowly fade, and anyone venturing into the wood is more likely to be greeted by the startled screech of a jay, the sudden wing-clapping of wood pigeons disturbed from their perches or the repetitive scolding of a blackbird. Pheasants may be flying to roost with throaty croaks and loud, drumming wingbeats, and as the darkness thickens, a sharp '*ke-wick*' announces the presence of that icon of the night, the tawny owl.

During the day, the tawny owl roosts quietly among the ivy-laden branches of tall trees.

Superbly camouflaged, it often remains motionless for hours on end in an attempt to avoid detection. The reason for its caution becomes clear as dusk falls and the hungry owl leaves its perch to look for prey. A number of small birds, intent on harassing the owl, fly around it, calling shrilly. While the evening light persists, the owl's assailants remain bold, but as the last glow of the setting sun fades from the sky they give up and leave the owl to its night patrol.

A skilled hunter, the tawny owl's sharp hearing enables it to pinpoint small mammals, its main prey, with ease.

▼ A roe buck emerges at dusk to feed. The thick grey-brown fur that roe deer grow in September is moulted into a sleek red coat in spring.

At sunset, daytime animals retire and nocturnal creatures emerge to feed. Soon the night air is alive with moths and other insects, and the bats that hunt them.

▲ The tawny owl relies on its highly developed senses to guide it through the dark woodland and detect its prey.

Its big dark eyes gather every glimmer of light, allowing it to navigate among the tree trunks and branches on moonless and starless nights that to human eyes seem pitch black. The tawny owl stays on the same territory throughout the year, so it knows all the best places to find food. It usually hunts from a series of favourite perches, listening for the telltale rustle or squeak of a potential meal.

Night sounds

The sounds of the woodland after dark are many and various, from the faint squeaks of shrews squabbling in the vegetation to the rustling of wood mice and bank voles scampering through the dry leaves on the woodland floor. Then there is the noise of hungry hedgehogs seeking a meal, snorting and snuffling up insects, worms and slugs.

The spines of hedgehogs protect them from owls, foxes and many other predators, yet they are not entirely safe in the dark. They may be caught by badgers, which emerge from their setts at dusk to feed. The badger eats a wide variety of plant and animal foods, including a lot of earthworms, but it is also an efficient hedgehog hunter. With its powerful forelimbs and long, stout claws, it is one

AUTUMN BATS

In early autumn the swarming insect life that takes to the night air attracts bats, which need to eat well before hibernating for the winter. The most spectacular is the powerful noctule, which can sometimes be seen flying high along open rides, then swooping down to snatch large insects from the air just above low vegetation. A far more common sight is the fast, fluttery flight of the tiny pipistrelle, which tends to hunt in clearings. The long-eared bat is a true woodland specialist. Its extremely agile flight style enables it to dodge around trunks and branches, and its finely tuned echo-location system allows it to detect insects among dense foliage, by distinguishing the difference between the quality of the echoes. It hovers among the foliage and plucks insects from leaves.

With its huge yet delicate ears, the long-eared bat is able to pick up the faintest sounds made by its prey.

▶ The loud squeaks of the fat dormouse resonate through the night in Chiltern beech woods. It resembles a small grey squirrel, but is nocturnal.

of the few animals capable of penetrating a hedgehog's defences, killing and eating it.

Glowing eyes

Like the tawny owl, most woodland mammals have sensitive night vision. The pupils of their large eyes open wide to collect as much of the dim light as possible, and focus it on cells that are adapted to detect low light levels rather than colours. The cells are arranged in a sheet called the retina, and a reflective layer behind the retina bounces any stray light back on to the cells to increase the stimulus. It is this reflective layer that causes the shine in the eyes of a nocturnal hunter caught in a torch's beam.

Good eyesight is as vital to the creatures that are preyed upon as it is to the hunters. Rabbits and deer have acute nocturnal vision, finely tuned to detect movement. This is of

little use in finding the plants on which they feed but, coupled with excellent hearing and a keen sense of smell, it helps them to evade their enemies.

For many animals, vision also plays an important role in communication, even at night. Contrasting patterns show up

▲ A hollow tree will provide a home for a little owl. Although often seen by day, it usually hunts by night, using a perch to watch and listen for prey.

▶ The wood mouse is active at night, often climbing trees in search of food. It looks out for predators, such as tawny owls, using its big eyes and ears.

well in low light, so bold stripes and patches, such as the black and white facial stripes of badgers or the bold throat patch of pine martens, probably act as recognition features between individuals in the gloom.

Hearing is important in communication between nocturnal animals. Most vocalisation between woodland mammals is restricted to gruff barks and occasional squeaks, but for some species sound signals are essential to finding a mate and holding a territory. During the fox's winter mating season, for example, the scream of a vixen carries far and wide through the still air of the woodland at night.

The vixen's scream is a familiar sound, unlike the loud, ascending squeaks of the fat dormouse.

This strange, yet unmistakable noise can be heard only in the dark beech woods of the northern Chilterns, where the species was deliberately introduced in 1902. Muntjac and sika deer also become surprisingly vocal as darkness falls, and the blood-curdling bark of an alarmed roe deer is enough to startle even the most hardened of wildlife watchers.

When night falls, young foxes emerge from their woodland dens to practise their hunting skills. Their keen senses of smell and hearing enable them to find prey even on the darkest nights.

Sweet scents

The senses of smell and touch are well developed in nocturnal mammals. Many species have long, touch-sensitive whiskers. These are particularly important to creatures that live in trees, such as the common or hazel dormouse, enabling them to feel their way through the dark as they climb through the woodland canopy in search of food. The sensitive nose of a dormouse enables it to detect the heavy, sweet scent of ripe fruits in the damp night air of autumn as it builds up its energy reserves in preparation for its winter hibernation.

In early autumn, the spicy scent of honeysuckle flowers may still hang heavy in the air, trapped by the foliage above. Many night-flying moths are irresistibly drawn

Woodland at night can be a dangerous place to walk. It is easy to become disorientated and then lost in unfamiliar surroundings in the dark. Also, the ground is often pitted with holes, ditches and even ponds, which can catch out the unwary. Be careful, tell someone where you are going and when you expect to be back, and don't go alone.

COOL COMFORT

Even in autumn, avoiding the heat of the day is vital for many small woodland creatures, because their thin, permeable skins expose them to the risk of rapid dehydration in the sun.

The bodies of leopard slugs, for example, are covered with slime to minimise water loss from the surface of their skin, but this provides little protection from the heat of the day. The slugs therefore retreat beneath rotting wood, leaf litter and damp vegetation during the day, and emerge only at night when the cool, moist woodland air provides them with ideal conditions for foraging and feeding. Warm, humid evenings also tempt

large numbers of earthworms to the surface. Under cover of darkness they are safe from the hungry birds that would seize them by day. However, they are not safe from the toads and frogs that also tend to emerge by night to avoid the sun, and eat large numbers of worms and slugs before slipping back into their daytime refuges.

◄ A woodland toad is most active at night when the cool, damp air enables it to move around freely, searching for earthworms.

► As night falls, millipedes emerge from beneath logs and debris to forage for food in the carpet of decaying leaf litter.

▲ Leopard slugs emerge only at night, when they browse on fungi or climb high into the tree canopy to eat algae growing on the trunks.

to the strong smell of these blooms. In some years, the second generation of large moths, such as the eyed and poplar hawk-moths, which require warmth to power their big flight muscles, forage soon after sunset while the air is still

warm. Later in the season, the night air of many woodlands is filled with male winter moths. These tiny insects are drawn by the scent of the wingless females, which crawl up the tree trunks to attract the males with their seductive perfume.

WILDLIFE WATCH

How can I watch woodland wildlife at night?

● Join a guided night visit at a local nature reserve where an experienced naturalist will help you to make the most of the experience.

● Whether being guided or visiting local woods independently, avoid wearing strong scents and clothes that make a noise when you move because these will alert animals and birds to your presence. Try not to move around too much in any case because the rustling of leaf litter and undergrowth will not only scare wildlife but also inhibit your own sense of hearing.

● Try to avoid using a torch because it may startle the creatures you have come to see, as well as ruining your night vision. Many nocturnal mammals cannot see red light, so if you do need to use a torch, place a red filter over the beam.

● Allow the creatures to come to you. Sit quietly and wait for your eyes to adjust to the low light level – a moonlit night is best – and listen for the changing sounds of the woods. Place yourself downwind of a clearing and tuck yourself close to a tree to break up your outline.

Badgers like to live in undisturbed woodland with well-drained soil that enables them to dig their setts easily. Plenty of food is usually available in such places, and at dusk the badgers emerge to forage for earthworms, slugs, insects and small mammals.

The New Forest – mosaic of woods and heath

In autumn, this wonderfully diverse national park – the newest in Britain – is ablaze with glorious colours. This is also the time of the annual deer ruts and wild pony round-ups.

Few major wildlife refuges are so misleadingly named as the New Forest. It was 'new' in the year 1079, when it was declared a royal deer preserve by William I, and at that time – and for many centuries afterwards – the word 'forest' had nothing to do with trees. It meant an area of land where deer were protected by law. A forest could be woodland, but it could also be grassland, moorland or heath. In fact, a large proportion of the New Forest is treeless heathland, and has been so for more than 1500 years thanks to the thin, acid soils that underlie the region. Where the original woodland was cleared by prehistoric farmers, grazing prevented the re-growth of trees on the poor soil, and they were replaced by great tracts of heather and grass. Meanwhile the woodland that had not been felled in prehistory survived into the medieval era. The woods were exploited for timber over many years, but natural regeneration preserved their wild character. Today many of these ancient woodlands still exist, with oaks, beeches and hollies of all ages.

The forest laws established by the Normans prevented local people from enclosing land or poaching deer, but allowed them certain rights to cut wood and graze their

animals. Some of these commoners' rights still exist today. From the late 17th century, however, many parts of the New Forest were enclosed for planting trees, initially oak for shipbuilding, setting a precedent for later conifer plantations. In March 2005 the whole area, covering some 570 sq km (220 sq miles), became a National Park, protecting it from further development.

Varied habitats

The legacy of this long history of varied land use is a rich variety of wildlife habitats. They include ancient broad-leaved woodlands, oak and conifer plantations, grasslands, heaths and valley bogs, interspersed with fields, farms and villages. In many woodlands regular grazing beneath the trees limits the ground cover and encourages

grass, creating wood-pasture. Damp, close-grazed 'lawns' of grass and moss have sprung up between the trees.

Much of the grazing land within the park is unfenced, allowing deer, sheep, cattle and the renowned New Forest ponies to roam freely over the landscape and its roads. This gives the area a pastoral charm that attracts millions of visitors a year. As summer gives way to the cool, misty days of autumn, the visitors thin out. The wild character of the landscape becomes more evident as it enters one of its most beautiful phases, especially in the broad-leaved woods where the foliage of the great trees turns to wonderful colours.

▶ A hobby may still be seen hunting over the New Forest in September, before it flies south to Africa for the winter.

Bramblings are winter visitors that start to arrive in mid-September. Small numbers usually feed among larger flocks of very similar-looking chaffinches.

New Forest ponies tend to congregate where there is food and where they can escape swarms of irritating flies. The ponies are rounded up every autumn for veterinary treatment, and stallions may be taken in for the winter.

The vegetation beneath beeches is relatively sparse because during the growing season the tree foliage intercepts most of the light. In autumn, however, the thinning of the canopy allows dappled sunlight to reach the forest floor.

The trees are visions in yellow, gold and red-brown before the leaves fall to create multi-coloured drifts on the ground.

A vast array of fungi sprout from the carpet of fallen leaves on the damp earth and from the rotting remains of fallen trees. The familiar mushrooms, toadstools and puffballs are the fruiting bodies of the fungi, the main parts of which form extensive networks of branching, thread-like filaments, or hyphae, in the soil and decaying timber. The combination of warmth and moisture typical of autumn is ideal for the germination of their spores.

Deer and ponies

Autumn is the rutting season for the red, fallow and sika deer that live in the forest. Red stags roar from the heaths, fallow bucks groan from the woods, and sika stags give loud shrieking whistles, each vying with rivals to attract females and mate with them. Of these three species, fallow

Shy and secretive, New Forest foxes feed on birds, rabbits and smaller mammals, but also raid litter bins. These young foxes are play-fighting.

deer are the most numerous in the New Forest, along with the smaller roe deer that rut earlier in the year, in summer.

The forest was originally set aside to protect deer, but today the most conspicuous large animals are the New Forest ponies. Some 3000 of them live semi-wild in the forest, roaming at will in search of good grazing. They are essentially identical to the wild ponies that lived in Britain some 2000 years ago, and may even be descended from that native stock.

Food larder

For many birds and small mammals, autumn is the time to stock up for the winter. Grey squirrels gather nuts, and jays spend much time collecting acorns and burying them in secret caches in the forest. The acorns provide jays with food throughout the winter, but while the birds retrieve most of them, some are forgotten and take root. In this way jays assist oaks by spreading their seeds.

The jay is a wary bird and usually flies off into cover with a loud screech when disturbed. Even less approachable is Britain's

largest resident member of the finch family, the hawfinch. The woods of the New Forest are home to a fair number of these elusive birds, which usually fly high into the trees with ticking alarm calls at the first sight of people. They favour woods where hollies grow beneath the oaks and beeches, and when the leaves are on the trees these birds are extremely difficult to observe. Autumn and winter offer a much better chance of a sighting, especially among hornbeam trees. Hawfinches use their huge, sturdy bills to crack open the hard hornbeam seeds.

Another bird that eats a lot of nuts and seeds in autumn is the nuthatch. It can often be seen jerkily working its way over the branches and trunks of broad-leaved trees, always moving headfirst regardless of whether it is going up or down.

The treecreeper has a similar foraging technique, although it feeds mainly on small insects and spiders. It spirals up a tree, using its slender, curved bill to probe for prey in crevices in the bark or among the lichens, mosses and ivy.

The great spotted woodpecker is also active in autumn. As it hacks into timber in search of wood-boring insect grubs, it makes an erratic hammering sound rather than the rapid drumming that it uses to attract a mate in spring.

Spectacular insects

Some of the grubs extracted by woodpeckers are those of stag beetles. The New Forest is home to one of the largest British populations of this declining species, which spends up to three years as a soft-bodied, burrowing larva feeding on rotten wood. It favours oak, so the older woodlands of the New Forest provide plenty of suitable timber. The adults emerge in summer, and the big males with their oversized jaws make an extraordinary sight when they take to the air on warm summer evenings in search of females. The adult beetles cannot eat solid food, and live for three or four weeks after emerging – just long enough to mate and lay their eggs.

An insect unique to the region is the New Forest cicada. Britain's only cicada, this insect has a lifecycle very

RARE REPTILES

Among the reptiles that live on New Forest heathland are the rare smooth snake and sand lizard, which are still active in early autumn. Both have declined considerably in recent decades. In fact the sand lizard became extinct in the New Forest but has recently been reintroduced.

▲ Smooth snakes are found on the heaths of the New Forest and in Dorset and Surrey, where they prey on lizards and small mammals.

◄ The sand lizard can sometimes be seen basking on a few south-facing sandy slopes. Breeding males have bright green flanks, which slowly fade during summer.

▲ The scarce blood foot fungus grows on the stumps of oak and beech trees. Some species of fungi have been so depleted by collectors that picking them is now illegal in some parts of the park.

▼ The rare Dartford warbler is resident all year round but suffers badly in unusually cold seasons. The grey crown, wine-red underparts and red eye indicate this one is a male.

▼ Red deer graze New Forest heaths but are not as numerous as the roe and fallow deer that live in the woodlands.

much like that of the stag beetle, spending years as a burrowing grub feeding on roots, and just a few days or weeks as an adult. It appears in May and June, and as the adults sit on trees the males produce the relentless whistling noise for which they are famous.

Several unusual butterflies live in the New Forest. The white admiral can be seen in woodlands and glades in summer, and the silver-washed fritillary perhaps as late as early September. The grayling and silver-studded blue live on open heaths. The magnificent emperor moth breeds on heather but is only on the wing in spring. Some 28 species of dragonflies and damselflies regularly breed in the heathland pools, including rarities such as keeled skimmer and black darter dragonflies, and the scarce blue damselfly.

Heathland birds

The New Forest heaths can be bleak, windswept places in late autumn and winter, but they come to life again in spring, when the air is full of bird song and the buzzing of insects. One of the most beautiful songs is that of the woodlark – a liquid, descending yodel accompanying a slow, circling display flight. The New Forest heaths are among the most important breeding sites of this scarce species.

The same is true of the Dartford warbler, one of the few warblers to stay in Britain all the year. A secretive bird, the Dartford warbler is difficult to locate as it skulks among gorse or tall heather, but its short churring alarm notes often betray its presence close by. Occasionally, males sing from the tops of bushes, perched with their long tails cocked up at a steep angle.

High overhead, hobbies hunt throughout the summer and early autumn. These dashing falcons rely on speed, and regularly catch swallows and even swifts, especially when feeding their young in August and September. They also feed on flying insects, catching them with their feet in mid-air, and when dragonflies are abundant it is possible to see half a dozen hobbies in the air at once.

Another insect eater is the nightjar, a summer visitor that hunts its airborne prey after dark. The male also gives vent to his weird, mechanical churring song at night, often for hours on end. By autumn most nightjars have left for their long journey back to Africa, but in early September a few may still be seen hunting above the heather at dusk, silhouetted against the darkening sky like giant swifts.

Places to visit in the New Forest

Almost anywhere in the New Forest can be worth visiting to search for wildlife, but it is worth getting away from the more popular areas near the car parks and exploring on foot. Special wildlife attractions and reserves include the following:

1 Blashford Lakes. These private gravel pits support a good range of wildlife with plenty of wildfowl in autumn and winter, and grebes and dragonflies in summer. They may be viewed from the surrounding roads and footpaths, and the Blashford Lakes Study Centre is available for pre-arranged school parties and community groups. For details, telephone 01425 472760.

2 Bolderwood Deer Sanctuary. A viewing platform provides excellent views of fallow deer. Bolderwood Walks take in a variety of wooded areas that are good for sighting redwings and fieldfares in late autumn/winter and a variety of breeding birds in spring/summer, including firecrests, hawfinches and crossbills.

3 Lymington-Keyhaven National Nature Reserve. This is a superb site for coastal birds, including many autumn migrant waders such as knots, sanderlings, curlew sandpipers, wood sandpipers, little stints and greenshanks. Winter brings more waders, including curlews, redshanks and grey plovers, plus ducks and brent geese. Short-eared owls, peregrines, merlins and hen harriers may also be seen at times from late autumn all through winter. Summer is an excellent time for terns. Hurst Spit and the sea wall footpath east from Keyhaven Marsh offer excellent viewpoints.

4 Lower Test Marshes Nature Reserve. At the head of Southampton Water, this reserve has breeding habitats that include salt marshes, reedbeds and wader scrapes. Two hides overlook the latter and footpaths give views over reedbeds. Plants range from sea aster to green-winged orchids. Migrant waders visit the scrape in spring and autumn, along with marsh harriers and ospreys, while reed and sedge warblers – and resident Cetti's warblers – can be seen in summer.

5 New Forest Nature Quest. This has a broad range of native British mammals and some domesticated species. Close encounters are guaranteed. It also carries out breeding programmes and research. Open to the general public and to school groups. For details, telephone 023 80292166.

6 Reptiliary at Holiday Hill. Specially constructed enclosures allow amazing views of the increasingly rare and elusive reptiles and amphibians of the New Forest. The displays detail what is being done to ensure their survival locally in the wild. Open from Easter to October.

● **New Forest Badger Watch**. Badgers can be viewed at close quarters at a secret location in the west of the New Forest. Directions for a one-hour evening visit are given when you book. Bookings are taken from 9.00am to 10am from 1 March to 31 October. For details, telephone 01425 403412.

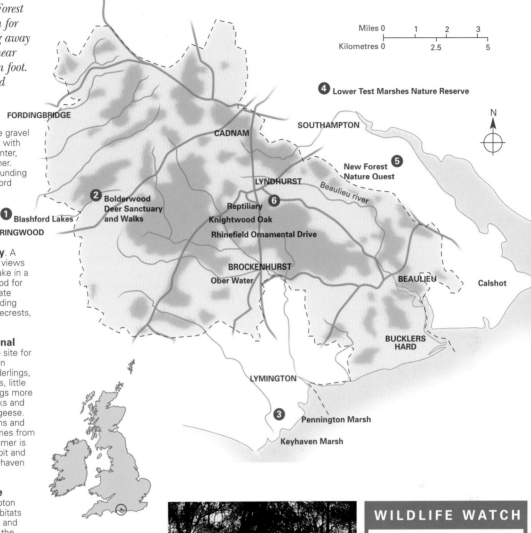

The varied terrain supports a diverse flora. The heath-spotted orchid thrives on the acid, peaty soils on the damper parts of the open heathland.

Grazing animals keep a check on undergrowth in the New Forest, allowing trees to grow to their full majesty. This has created some of Britain's most attractive nature walks and rides.

WILDLIFE WATCH

How can I find out more about the New Forest?

Further information can be obtained from:

● Forest Enterprise (England), The Queen's House, Lyndhurst, Hampshire SO43 7NH. Telephone 023 80283141 or visit www.forestry.gov.uk

● Hampshire and Isle of Wight Wildlife Trust, Beechcroft House, Vicarage Lane, Curdridge, Hampshire SO32 2DP. Telephone 01489 774400 or visit www.hwt.org.uk

● New Forest National Park Authority, The Queen's House, 4 High Street, Lyndhurst, Hampshire SO43 7BD. Telephone 023 80284144 or visit www.newforestnpa.gov.uk

Animals and plants in focus

Grassland watch

- The harvest mouse
- The pygmy shrew
- The little owl
- The magpie
- Spinners of silk
- The harvestmen
- Wild berries
- Nightshades
- Recognising grassland fungi

The harvest mouse

Often overlooked in summer among the tall grasses of field margins and reedbeds, the tiny harvest mouse is more easily seen when the vegetation dies down and it goes in search of winter quarters closer to the ground.

As its name implies, the harvest mouse has long been associated with ripe, golden cornfields. In the days when corn was cut by hand, these mice would be seen scampering out of the way during the harvest – the peak time for this smallest of European rodents as a result of numerous litters raised during the summer.

The Reverend Gilbert White, a renowned 18th-century naturalist, was the first to identify the species officially. He lived in Selborne in Hampshire and found the mouse living in cornfields around the village. Once people started to look for it, the mouse was found to be widespread throughout Britain. It is so tiny and unobtrusive, though, that it easily escapes notice and by the early 20th century, a lack of sightings led many naturalists to suggest it was dying out.

One reason for this, however, was that people were looking for harvest mice in the wrong places. The assumption that cornfields were the main habitat of these creatures was reinforced by countless drawings and photographs of them posed among corn stems. In fact, they have never established permanent populations in corn because the crop is removed every year. Each new crop needs to be re-invaded by mice from somewhere else. This 'somewhere else' is their permanent home and the best place to look for them.

Grasses and reeds

In summer, harvest mice are at home in tall grasses and weeds. They scramble about like miniature monkeys among the stems and leaves, building their summer nests off the ground. As well as cornfields

they inhabit tussocks of sedges and grasses – cock's-foot is a favourite – hedge bases and marshland with tall vegetation. They will even live in reedbeds over standing water and in the long grass and bramble patches of wasteground.

Population surveys

In the early 1970s, conservationists organised surveys to look for harvest mice and the animal was quickly rediscovered, even in several parts of the Greater London area where it had previously been thought to be extinct.

The agile harvest mouse can easily climb up thin stems to get to food that heavier animals cannot reach. It searches for insects, pollen and seeds among the flowers and stalks.

HARVEST MOUSE FACT FILE

The harvest mouse has a pure white underside that contrasts sharply with the bright orange-chestnut fur on its back. In autumn, the upper fur begins to lose its warm tones and turns a darker brown to provide better camouflage.

● **NAMES**
Common name: harvest mouse
Scientific name: *Micromys minutus*

● **HABITAT**
Ungrazed hay meadows and other places with tall, stiff-stemmed weeds and long grass; hedge bases, reedbeds and edges of cornfields

● **DISTRIBUTION**
Widespread but patchy in southern and eastern England, scarcer in the north, especially the north-west; present in a few areas of Wales, mainly coastal; very few in Scotland; absent from Ireland

● **STATUS**
Around 1,415,000 in England, plus 10,000 in Wales

● **SIZE**
Length of head and body 50–70mm (2–2¾in); tail about 60mm (2⅜in); ear about 9mm (⅜in) long; weight of adult averages about 6g (¼oz)

● **KEY FEATURES**
Tiny, agile mouse; fur russet-orange, white underside well-delineated; nose blunt; ears small and hairy; tail tip prehensile (adapted for gripping), a feature that is unique among European mammals

● **HABITS**
Climbs stems of tall grasses, reeds and similar vegetation; in winter may descend to ground and occupy burrows; active mainly at night, sometimes during day, especially in summer

● **VOICE**
Occasional squeaks

● **FOOD**
Seeds (including cereal grains), green shoots in spring, small fruits, insects (especially in summer)

● **BREEDING**
Breeds from May until October, but sometimes as late as December if weather is mild; most litters born August–September; average litter 6, occasionally 8 or more

● **NEST**
Woven ball of shredded grass, about the size of a tennis ball

● **YOUNG**
Born naked; fine fur grows after 4 days; eyes open after 8 or 9 days; independent at around 14 days. Fur distinctly greyer than adults', otherwise similar. Mature at 35 days

● **SIGNS**
Distinctive spherical nests woven in tall vegetation, otherwise easily overlooked

Often weighing less than a two-pence coin, the diminutive harvest mouse is smaller and almost as light as a dandelion seedhead.

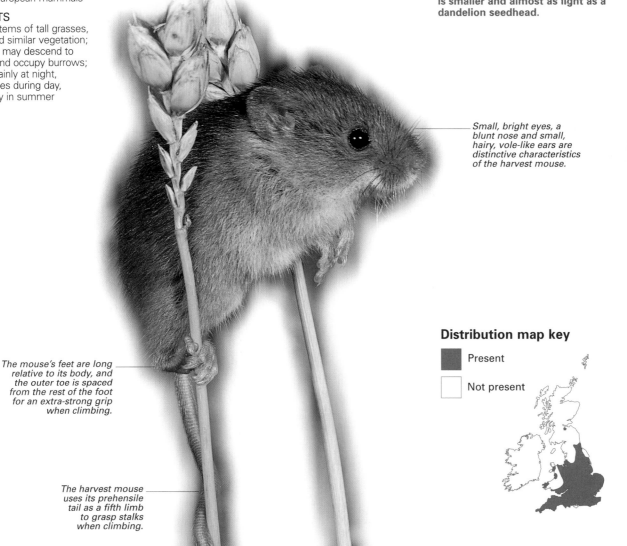

Small, bright eyes, a blunt nose and small, hairy, vole-like ears are distinctive characteristics of the harvest mouse.

The mouse's feet are long relative to its body, and the outer toe is spaced from the rest of the foot for an extra-strong grip when climbing.

The harvest mouse uses its prehensile tail as a fifth limb to grasp stalks when climbing.

Distribution map key

■ Present

☐ Not present

The Mammal Society carried out a national survey that confirmed harvest mice were common in many areas, including some places in Scotland and Wales where it had not been thought to live. The harvest mouse was not rare, as was feared – it had simply been overlooked.

When this survey was repeated 20 years later, in 1996–97, the picture was not so rosy. Field ecologists revisited over 800 of the places where harvest mice had been found in the 1970s to see if they were still there. Evidence of them was found in only about a quarter of the sites. The worst losses were in the cornfields of southern England, where more than 80 per cent of the former sites no longer had harvest mice present.

However, a number of more recent, localised surveys have produced conflicting results. Some suggest there has been a major decline over the last 30 years, others that the harvest mouse is actually far more common than previously thought. One such survey carried out in Essex, for example, found nests throughout the county, often about a kilometre (just over half a mile) away from previous sites. The harvest mice had merely moved to more suitable areas.

The decline recorded in the 1996–97 survey mirrors the growth in intensive farming and consequent destruction of habitat. However, the harvest mouse may be adapting and until another nationwide survey is carried out, searching for new places that the harvest mouse may have colonised, it is hard to be sure of its status. It may turn out to be under-recorded after all, especially taking into account annual population fluctuations.

Changing habitat

Hedges are ideal places for harvest mice to live, but many have been removed to make the bigger fields that are necessary to accommodate larger tractors. Boggy areas with reeds and tall-stemmed plants, also ideal for harvest mice, have been

◀ Juicy berries form an important part of the harvest mouse's diet. The small insects the berries attract, such as fruit flies, are an additional, protein-rich source of food.

▼ In hedgerows and at the edge of wooded areas, a harvest mouse may come across new sources of food, such as fungi, as it clambers among the twigs and branches.

During the autumn and early winter, seeds of rushes, grasses and other plants provide the harvest mouse with a rich source of energy to help sustain it during the cold weather to come.

drained to provide more land for growing crops. Weedy field corners and edges have gone under the plough as a result of farming subsidies that encourage grain production. Weedkillers remove many plants that are good for harvest mice, while insecticides destroy an important part of their food. So, far from being an ideal habitat for harvest mice, cornfields have become one of the least likely areas where the mice can survive.

Away from arable fields, large areas of grazing land remain. However, most of this land is now grazed intensively, right to the edges, and not much tall, grassy vegetation survives. Any that remains is generally too short for harvest mice. Grassy fields that used to be grazed occasionally, or were perhaps mown for hay once a year, are now scarce. Previously such fields were common and harboured large numbers of harvest mice.

Much 'wasteland', often good for small rodents, has disappeared under housing estates and industrial developments, while road widening has destroyed many weedy verges. Others are regularly mown or treated with herbicide, again spoiling them for mice.

Despite all these hazards, there are grounds for optimism for the harvest mouse. Recent developments may well result in the restoration of suitable habitat. New protection for hedgerows, for instance, and various types of set-aside farming arrangements, whereby land is left fallow, should provide places for them to live, at least along the edges of fields. Another helpful factor is that less money is being allocated for land drainage.

A light and agile climber

Although traditionally associated with cereal crops, the harvest mouse lives and breeds in any tall grass. It is so tiny that it can climb swiftly and confidently among the slender stalks and flowers.

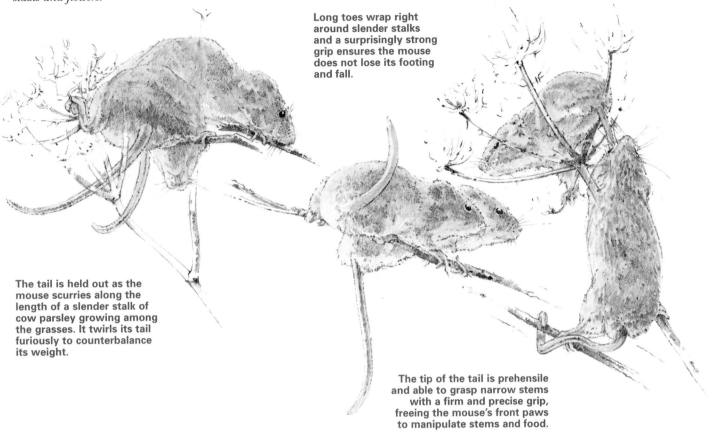

Long toes wrap right around slender stalks and a surprisingly strong grip ensures the mouse does not lose its footing and fall.

The tail is held out as the mouse scurries along the length of a slender stalk of cow parsley growing among the grasses. It twirls its tail furiously to counterbalance its weight.

The tip of the tail is prehensile and able to grasp narrow stems with a firm and precise grip, freeing the mouse's front paws to manipulate stems and food.

NEST BUILDERS

The harvest mouse is the only British mammal to build its nest in tall grass, typically 30–60cm (1–2ft) above the ground. In tall reeds, nests may be sited higher still.

About the size of a tennis ball, the nest is woven from the shredded leaves of adjacent grasses. The mouse, sitting at the base of a leaf, pulls other leaves through its teeth to shred them. When enough are ready, it weaves them into a hollow ball, pulling more leaves inside through the walls of the nest. Once inside, these leaves are also shredded and incorporated into the structure while remaining attached to the grass stems outside.

Harvest mice particularly favour cock's-foot grass in which to nest. This forms tall tussocks and is used for about three-quarters of all harvest mouse nests.

These nests, built up among tall stalks, are used in summer, larger ones for breeding and smaller, loosely woven ones – about 5cm (2in) in diameter – for sleeping in. Breeding nests are tightly woven and often lined with very finely

chewed grass or even specially collected thistledown. Each litter has a new nest.

When the nests are first constructed, they are hard to spot because they are made of living grass and are green, just like all the surroundings. In autumn, when the grass withers, the nests become easier to see, but by then they are usually empty because the mice have left for their winter quarters.

In winter, harvest mice build small nests, low to the ground and deep within grass tussocks. These nests are more difficult to find.

An artificial nest for a harvest mouse can be made out of an old tennis ball nailed some way up a stick, which is then pushed into the ground among tall grass. The entrance hole needs to be about 15mm (⅝in) in diameter. Harvest mice will set up home in them, just as birds use nestboxes.

▶ A harvest mouse's nest remains secure because some of the leaves that form an integral part of it are still attached to the grass or corn stem.

Grain forms a major part of the diet of the harvest mouse, but since the amount eaten is negligible, this rodent has never been persecuted by farmers. In fact, the mice help farmers by eating insects such as aphids.

It remains to be seen to what extent this tiny animal is able to recolonise lost ground. Harvest mice normally travel short distances only, and rarely move far from where they were born. Recolonisation may take a long time, unless aided by deliberate reintroductions. In some parts of Cheshire, this is already under way.

Avoiding predators

In summer, harvest mice tend to spend much of their time up among the stalks of grasses and other plants, where it is difficult for predators to catch them. At the slightest threat, the mouse can leap to the ground and disappear into the

A USEFUL TAIL

The harvest mouse has a prehensile tail. It can wrap the tip around thin objects to support its weight and can even hang by its tail, not needing any other support. This is especially useful when the animal is scrambling among stems of grasses that are swaying in the wind.

Holding on by its tail steadies the mouse and reduces the risk of falling off. Getting a grip with its tail also allows the mouse to let go with its front paws, which it can then use like hands for other purposes, such as collecting food or gathering nest materials. When moving rapidly among grass stems, the tail is flicked from side to side to help maintain the mouse's balance.

▶ A gripping tail is a feature that the harvest mouse shares with some South American monkeys but relatively few other mammals around the world and none in Europe.

thick grass, although where harvest mice become numerous, barn owls, major predators of all types of mice, may quickly learn to catch them and consume considerable numbers.

When the vegetation dies back during the autumn, harvest mice build winter nests low to the ground in grassy tussocks. They may also take up residence in the tunnels and burrows made by other small mammals. These provide shelter until new vegetation grows in spring and the mice can move back among the stalks. Harvest mice are particularly vulnerable in the autumn and winter, when there is little vegetation to provide cover, and they may seek refuge in barns and outhouses.

As well as owls, harvest mice are hunted by weasels and cats, but on the whole they are too small to interest many of the usual

larger predators. Being so tiny, however, they are vulnerable to attack from unexpected quarters, such as crows, blackbirds and even toads.

Surviving the weather

The harvest mouse's size is a disadvantage in cold weather. Small animals find it more difficult to maintain their body temperature than larger ones and sharp frosts in the autumn reduce the population substantially. Juveniles are especially vulnerable. Persistent rain batters down the tall grass stems, wrecking the harvest mouse's home, and heavy dew wets everything, threatening to clog the

▲ A female harvest mouse is pregnant for 17 to 19 days and the average family consists of six to eight minute babies. The mother, weighing only about 6g (¼oz) after giving birth, supports all these babies using just her own milk.

◀ After mating, the mice split up and the male plays no part in raising his family. Harvest mice do not form social groups but do tend to be tolerant of each other.

fur of these tiny creatures. This may cause them to lose body heat and die. Small wonder that most harvest mice do not live longer than six months.

Harvest mice make up for such inevitable losses by prolific breeding. This begins in May and continues into the autumn. About three-quarters of the young are born in August and September, when the weather is generally dry and warm. Babies that are born in late autumn may be overtaken by bad weather and many die in the nest or soon after leaving home.

A litter consists of up to eight young although as many as 12 have been reported. Most of the adults that have bred during the summer die soon afterwards, presumably because breeding is such a strain on them. Those that live longest are individuals that are born late in the year but escape bad weather, and do not breed until the following season. Some of these animals may live to be 18 months old, although this is very unusual. In captivity, safe from predators and severe weather, harvest mice have been known to live for five years.

▲ The harvest mouse is often active during the day as well as at night, which makes it a target of birds that feed in the daytime, such as this carrion crow.

Although the harvest mouse's vision is not particularly good, its bright eyes can detect movement and its acute hearing warns it of danger.

The young weigh about 0.7g (a fraction of an ounce) at birth but grow extraordinarily fast. Fine, downy fur begins to grow on the fourth day and eyes open on the eighth or ninth day after birth. The babies begin to leave the nest and explore their surroundings when they are around 11 days old, and the mother abandons her family after they are weaned at around two weeks old. By this time, the female is often pregnant again. She then builds a new breeding nest nearby and raises another family.

Population explosion

A single female may have many families during the summer and early autumn. Some of the young will breed, which they can do at five weeks old, and their offspring may themselves be breeding before the summer is out. Populations can build up to high levels in the autumn, especially if cold weather is delayed until October or November, allowing time to raise yet more young. At this time, some fields may appear to be seething with harvest mice. Many will die over winter, however, as the weather worsens and food supplies dwindle. Harvest mice do not hibernate but stay close the ground, where it is warmer.

WILDLIFE WATCH

Where can I see harvest mice?

● Southern England is the best place to look for harvest mice. The nests are far easier to find than the actual animals. Look in field corners with long grass – more than knee high. Search the dead grasses at the foot of old hedges, and low brambles at the edge of fields with permanent grass.

● Nests are most numerous in early autumn when the vegetation is still standing tall. Later when the grasses collapse, nests are harder to find but the harvest mice themselves may be seen as they are forced to travel along the ground, often in daylight. Later in the winter, mortality will take its toll and the animals will be fewer and seen less often.

Adults do not move around very much, having a home range of around 300 to 600 square metres (3200–6500sq ft), which is equivalent to a circle about 19–38m (60–125ft) in diameter. Ranges overlap, which indicates that the species is not territorial, and in captivity they tolerate living very closely together.

In the spring, harvest mice may explore new areas in which to live. Even so, they rarely move more than 100m (330ft) or so from where they were born and prefer to travel along hedges and weed-fringed ditches, where they can clamber about in the relative safety of dense vegetation. As the grasses begin to grow tall, the young adults begin constructing new breeding nests and the cycle starts all over again.

The pygmy shrew

Little bigger than a stag beetle, the pygmy shrew has to eat more than its own body weight every day just to stay alive – and consequently rarely sleeps for more than a few minutes at a time.

In the autumn, when many animals are preparing to hibernate, it is business as usual for the pygmy shrew. Unlike hedgehogs or dormice, it cannot conserve energy during food shortages or very cold weather by becoming torpid (slowing down all bodily functions so that the heart just ticks over). Instead, the pygmy shrew has to stay active and warm all year round. In fact, it will starve if it does not eat at least every two hours.

The pygmy shrew is tiny, with a head and body measuring just 64mm (2½in) long at most. You might expect such a small creature to be very delicate, managing to survive only in sheltered places. However, this is miniaturisation at its best, for the pygmy shrew is not only one of the world's smallest mammals, but also one of the most successful. It is found throughout Britain and all across Europe, east to Siberia and north into the Arctic.

Conserving body heat

A particular problem for such a small warm-blooded animal is how to avoid losing precious body heat. Small mammals have a bigger surface area in proportion to their bulk than larger ones and so lose heat rapidly. A pygmy shrew loses heat far more quickly than, say, a rat or a dog, and is always on the limit of survival. Some mammals prevent heat loss by growing longer hair for the winter to insulate themselves against the cold but this is not an option for the pygmy shrew.

Endless curiosity and a long, pointed nose are the pygmy shrew's main assets when it comes to finding food. Its long, fine whiskers are sensitive to the tiniest vibrations, picking up any movement nearby.

TREE CLIMBERS

Pygmy shrews are quite often found in nestboxes put up for birds or dormice, over 1.5m (5ft) off the ground. Climbing trees and bushes is perhaps an unexpected activity for animals that are generally thought to be ground-dwellers, but shrews do not nest or breed in the boxes. They probably find them a treasure trove of food, from moths to spiders and woodlice, many of which use empty nestboxes as convenient daytime shelters.

PYGMY SHREW FACT FILE

Adept at remaining under cover, the pygmy shrew is a silent forager. When it does appear it can be distinguished from its more numerous cousin, the common shrew, by its tiny size and its bulbous head.

● **NAMES**
Common name: pygmy shrew
Scientific name: *Sorex minutus*

● **HABITAT**
Prefers grassland, but also heaths, farmland, hedgerows, woodland edges and moorland

● **DISTRIBUTION**
Throughout mainland Britain and Ireland; present on many offshore islands but absent from Shetland and Isles of Scilly

● **STATUS**
Very common. Population estimated at about 6–8 million

● **SIZE**
Length of head and body 40–64mm (1½–2½in), tail 30–45mm (1¼–1¾in); weight 2.5–6g (less than ¼oz)

● **KEY FEATURES**
Fur brown, darker above, paler from flanks downwards; tail thick and almost as long as head and body; head bulbous; ears small, hidden in fur; eyes tiny, black; nose long, narrow and pointed; teeth tipped with red

● **HABITS**
Active day and night, in long grass and under shrubbery; solitary except when mating

● **VOICE**
Loud shrill squeak if alarmed

● **FOOD**
Small invertebrates especially beetles, woodlice, spiders and snails

● **BREEDING**
Usually two litters per season, each of 4–7 young, born mainly April–August but occasionally as late as October, peaking in June

● **NEST**
Small ball of grass or leaves, usually located in a burrow, under a log or in other shelter

● **YOUNG**
Less distinct demarcation between upper and underside fur colour than in adult; tail even more hairy than adult's, especially along middle section, which appears bushy as a result

● **SIGNS**
Tiny footprints in mud; tiny dark droppings

The long nose of the pgymy shrew, with its abundant coating of whiskers, contributes as much through the sense of touch as smell, and also through its sensitivity to vibration.

Distribution map key

Present

Not present

Long sensitive whiskers help the shrew to detect its prey.

Tiny ears hidden in fur pick up the sounds of insects.

The bulbous head has no obvious neck.

Short, velvety fur helps the shrew to keep warm.

The hairy tail looks thicker than that of the common shrew.

PROTECTED!

All shrews have partial protection under Schedule 6 of the Wildlife and Countryside Act, 1981. They may not be deliberately trapped or killed without a special license.

When a shrew comes across an area where prey is plentiful, it will concentrate its foraging efforts there. It thrusts its nose under leaves and into crevices, seeking out any small invertebrates that may be hiding there.

Hairs as long as would be needed to retain heat would get in the way and hinder movement, so when the pygmy shrew moults in the autumn and grows its winter coat, the length of its fur does not increase much more than its usual 3mm (⅛in). Yet somehow the animal manages to survive in very cold places.

The autumn moult starts on the rump and proceeds forwards to the nose. In spring the reverse takes place, the moult back to a summer coat starting on the head and finishing on the tail. How these forward and backward waves of moulting and new hair growth are controlled remains a mystery.

The shrew grooms its fur regularly to ensure that it is able to retain the maximum amount of body heat. Despite such close attention to personal hygiene, however, pygmy shrews only temporarily rid themselves of parasites such as ticks, mites and fleas.

High energy intake

Pygmy shrews escape from the cooling effects of the wind by remaining under cover for as much of the time as possible, which also reduces the danger from predators. However, their main defence against becoming fatally chilled is to produce more heat. Their metabolic rate is enormously high and they burn up huge amounts of energy all the time. For every gram of bodyweight, the energy consumption of a shrew is about 10 times that of a rat and 65 times that of a horse.

Producing all this energy means that the shrew must feed almost continuously in order to maintain the supplies of fuel needed to keep its body going. It must eat 25 per cent more than its own bodyweight every day – the equivalent of a 60kg (9½ stone) human consuming 75kg (12 stone) of food daily. Fortunately, the efficiency of the pygmy shrew's digestive system is greater than that of larger mammals, so it does at least make the most of its food.

Rival shrews

The pygmy shrew eats a lot of spiders, beetles and woodlice, taking far fewer slugs and worms than its relative, the common shrew. This reflects an important difference in the hunting techniques of the two species. Common shrews feed mainly inside their burrows on prey that inhabits the surrounding soil. Pygmy shrews, in contrast, feed on surface-dwelling invertebrates, especially spiders that lurk among the vegetation.

Foraging for food

Shrews cannot afford to leave any food they come across and will eat more or less any prey that they can kill. A pygmy shrew's diet consists of at least 35 different types of invertebrates and at any one time its stomach may contain the remains of more than a dozen different items.

Shrew teeth are tipped with red, caused by deposits of iron oxide in the tooth enamel, giving them a bloodthirsty appearance when the animal is feeding.

Although earthworms are not the pygmy shrew's main food item, it will attack with gusto any worms found on the surface, using its feet and jaws to pin down the prey.

A well-placed bite will render the outsize meal immobile.

▲ Despite its size, the pygmy shrew is a hardy creature that is perfectly capable of withstanding the harsh conditions of open land. It finds shelter in the tiny fissures that traverse rocky outcrops.

UNUSUAL HABIT

Shrews indulge in a strange activity known as 'refection', that is the eating and redigestion of incompletely digested food. The animal twists itself round so that it can lick its own anus. The rectum is protruded, sometimes by several millimetres, and a whitish fluid is excreted, which the shrew consumes.

The fluid seems to collect in the gut only when there is no food there to be digested, so it is not the same as faeces.

The process may be a way of recycling vitamins or other valuable substances in order to make up for deficiencies in the diet.

▼ The shrew curls into an inelegant ball in order to lick its anus. The precise purpose of this odd behaviour is not fully understood, but it is more to do with diet than grooming.

The difference in hunting strategy means that the common shrew is not well suited to living in places where there are few soil animals. This is probably a major reason why they like to live in grassland and woodland where they outnumber their smaller relatives by about six to one. Nevertheless, pygmy shrews thrive in this environment and in late summer and early autumn they may reach population densities of 10–12 per hectare (4–5 per acre) in grassy lowland areas.

On mountains and moorlands pygmy shrews tend to be more numerous than their cousin – few worms are to be found out on the moors but plenty of spiders and beetles. Both species live among sand dunes and here the common shrew again outnumbers the pygmy shrew, this time by two to one.

The shrew pins larger prey such as garden snails to the ground using its forepaws, while delivering repeated attacks with its teeth. Juicy food items such as this also provide the shrew with water.

Despite the common shrew being bigger and more numerous, the pygmy shrew is in no danger of being ousted because the two species do not compete for food or shelter.

Pygmy shrews are active throughout the day and night, unlike common shrews, which prefer to forage at night, and they inhabit larger home territories, often more than 1500 square metres (16,000 sq ft) in extent and bigger in winter than in summer. Pygmies spend about half their time on the surface, scurrying here and there in search of

food, and the other half underground. Common shrews spend only about 20 per cent of their time above ground.

Although less aggressive than common shrews, pygmies will usually try to keep intruders out of their territory. They avoid contact with others, except during the mating season, but if they do run into one another, they emit a sharp '*chit*' sound before moving off in different directions. Sometimes the encounter becomes more challenging and the shrews may lash their tails from side to side in an angry display that can escalate into a brief fight.

▼ Rearing up on its hind legs in order to sniff the air enables the pygmy shrew to detect the whereabouts of potential rivals, possible mates and predators.

◄ The business of foraging means the pygmy shrew is on the move most of the time, mainly under cover. Those shrews found dead in the open have usually been dropped there by predators.

▲ Resting consists of short naps lasting just a few minutes. Longer periods of inactivity take place in the shelter of the nest, but even then the shrew cannot afford to snooze for long, needing to continue its relentless search for food.

Food and water

As well as losing body heat, very small animals have a problem with losing moisture from the body. Rapid ventilation of the lungs results in a lot of water vapour being breathed out. Some of this can be replaced by water gained from food, but shrews also need to lap up dew or drops of rain.

Pygmy shrews do not appear to hunt systematically or search deliberately, but simply rush about in the hope and expectation of frequently finding something edible. Around 85 per cent of their prey items are tiny, less than 10mm (⅜in) long, and the shrew's poor eyesight is probably of little use in helping it to detect food. Its sense of smell is not particularly well developed, either.

Despite being a convenient bite size, a pygmy shrew is often too small to be worth catching for birds of prey. These shrews deter mammalian predators with their distasteful skin secretions, a defensive feature shared with other shrew species.

Common shrews have been known to locate insect pupae buried under 12cm (5in) of soil but pygmy shrews are not as good at finding things by smell alone.

The sound that spiders and other invertebrates make as they move among the undergrowth is probably the main indicator of their presence to a pygmy shrew. Its long whiskers are also very useful because with these the shrew can detect movements in the grass and among dense vegetation. To human ears, a spider is silent but close up the shrew hears faint rustling noises and feels the trembling of grass stems and leaves as the insect moves.

Once a spider has been located, the shrew will suddenly leap upon it, biting it furiously until it is dead. If the shrew comes across a beetle, it uses its sharp teeth to break through the creature's hard outer covering and may need to inflict many bites in order to kill its prey.

Home for one

A pygmy shrew's nest, which is not much bigger than a golf ball, is usually sited underground, or sometimes hidden in dense cover, and is accessed by several tunnels. Shrews may make these burrows themselves but they mostly use tunnels dug by other small mammals or cavities left by rotting tree roots.

The nests are constructed out of fine grasses, moss and leaves, with no special lining. When the breeding season begins, at around Easter time in the year following their birth, female shrews start to enlarge their nests in readiness for their first litters. Male pygmy shrews do not help with family duties and do not even share the same nest. The female raises the young alone.

Breeding cycle

Most females bear two litters during the season, but some may produce more. Breeding usually continues until the end of August but may occasionally carry on after then, on rare occasions even into October. The female is pregnant for 22 to 25 days and then gives birth to up to seven young. The babies are minute, weighing just a quarter of a gram, but they grow very rapidly on their mother's milk, increasing their size ten-fold within just two weeks.

Young pygmy shrews are independent at about three weeks old. They are not social creatures and each one leaves the nest on its own to establish a separate territory.

DID YOU KNOW?

● A pygmy shrew weighs less than a 20p coin or two lumps of sugar.

● A pygmy shrew's heart may beat more than 250 times a minute.

● An active pygmy shrew takes 200 breaths a minute.

As they reach adulthood, the young that survive the winter lose the extra long hairs from their tail that they grew as juveniles. This is almost the only outward sign of maturation. Whereas common shrews develop darker fur as they mature, in pygmy shrews the fur colour remains the same throughout life.

Shrew mortality

Like other small mammals, pygmy shrews are in some danger from predators, but they form only about 5 per cent of the diet of owls and other birds of prey. Most pygmy shrews probably die of cold or starvation. Mortality is particularly high during frosts when prey is hard to find, and also in wet weather when damp fur results in a high loss of precious body heat.

These tiny animals are living at the very edge of what is possible for a small, warm-blooded creature, so any additional problems with heat loss are likely to be fatal. About half of all pygmy shrews die within four months of birth. Roughly one in five survive long enough to breed, but virtually none live more than a year. The maximum age recorded is 13 months in the wild and 16 months in captivity.

The pygmy shrew colonises all types of habitat but prefers thick grassland vegetation, where it can scurry about unhindered in its constant pursuit of food.

Disproportionately long legs and large feet make the pygmy shrew very agile. These creatures will tackle uneven terrain and dense vegetation, and even climb trees.

WILDLIFE WATCH

Where can I see pygmy shrews?

● Pygmy shrews are not easy to find. Look for their nests in cavities under stones, among fallen trees, in rotten tree stumps and among dense ground vegetation. The nests, which are ball-shaped and made of moss, dried grass and other plant materials, are similar to those of the common shrew and other small rodents.

● Tiny footprints in mud, or snow, are another sign of a pygmy shrew's presence, especially if they are accompanied by a winding trail made by the tail. The tracks of pygmy and common shrews are almost the same, and can be distinguished from those made

by mice by the claw-marks – shrews have five claws and mice only four.

● Look for droppings under stones or pieces of wood. The droppings are very small, 2–4mm (less than ⅛in) long, and usually black or dark brown. They are often pointed at the ends and consist largely of insect remains.

● You are much more likely to see a pygmy shrew dead than alive. Their remains can sometimes be found in owl pellets or inside discarded bottles where they have crawled in search of food or water – one more reason for always taking your litter home.

The little owl

Prominent pale 'eyebrows' give the little owl a perpetually alarmed expression. Its big eyes with their unflinching gaze enable the bird to detect the smallest movement on the ground, either from a perch or as it flies swift and low over farmland.

On a warm, autumn evening, a sharp 'kiew' may echo through the air as a little owl wings it way over open grassland to its regular perch. The call, which is repeated at irregular, widely spaced intervals, is sometimes interspersed with an excited yelping 'werrow'.

Today the little owl is the second most common owl in Britain. It was deliberately introduced from continental Europe in the 19th century, when naturalists saw nothing wrong with introducing foreign species into the wild and no laws restricted the practice. Animal dealers regularly brought little owls across the Channel for sale as household pets – apparently they were great cockroach killers – and so it was not too difficult to obtain birds for release.

Little owls were set free in Yorkshire in the 1840s and later in Northamptonshire, Hampshire and Kent. The later releases appear to have led to the establishment of little owls as breeding residents.

Steady numbers

The first little owl nest was observed in Northamptonshire in 1889, after which these birds spread rapidly. By 1920, they had reached every English county south of the Humber and also much of Wales.

Having spotted potential prey, a little owl hovers above the ground, its wings spread wide and forwards. It usually hunts at dawn and dusk.

WISE OWL

Owls are widely regarded as symbols of wisdom, which may be attributed to their upright posture and amazingly attentive stare. Alternatively, it may be because their golden, apparently all-seeing eyes face forward, as human eyes do, rather than to the sides like those of many other birds.

In classical mythology, a little owl was the symbol of Pallas Athene, who was the patron of Athens and goddess of wisdom. The bird has been identified from coins of the time and the legend is commemorated in the modern scientific name for the little owl, *Athene noctua*. So it appears that this really is the original 'wise old owl'.

◄ With large eyes and unflinching gaze, the little owl can appear to be frowning or surprised, depending on whether its 'eyebrows' are raised or lowered.

LITTLE OWL FACT FILE

The little owl has longer legs, relative to its size, than any other British owl. It may occasionally be seen by day, perched upright and motionless on a tree branch, its spotted brown and buff plumage camouflaging it against its background.

● **NAMES**
Common name: little owl
Scientific name: *Athene noctua*

● **HABITAT**
Open country, especially farmland, rocky places and wasteland

● **DISTRIBUTION**
England, Wales, extreme south of Scotland

● **STATUS**
Despite cyclical changes, probably fairly stable; 6000–12,000 breeding pairs

● **SIZE**
Length 22cm (9in); weight 140–225g (5–8oz)

● **KEY FEATURES**
Small and squat with long legs, brown-and-white mottled plumage, yellow eyes and prominent 'eyebrows'; active by day as well as night; bobs up and down if alarmed or curious; can rotate its head upside down

● **HABITS**
Hunts mainly from dusk to midnight then, after a pause, until dawn, but may be seen during the day; its flight is swift, low and undulating

● **VOICE**
Shrill, plaintive *'kiew'*, repeated mournful *'gooeek'* spring song of male and barking *'werrow'* when alarmed or excited

● **FOOD**
Chiefly insects, plus small mammals, birds and earthworms

● **BREEDING**
April–May; one brood per season

● **NEST**
In tree hole or simple scrape in ruins, cliffs, burrows; will use nestboxes

● **EGGS**
3–5 white eggs; incubated by female; hatch in 28–29 days

● **YOUNG**
Nestlings have short, white down; male brings food at first, later both parents hunt for them; fledge after 30–35 days

In common with other owls, little owls usually swallow prey whole. Bones and insect wings are then separated from the soft parts in the owl's stomach and regurgitated as pellets, which may collect under a regular perch.

Distribution map key

■ Present all year round

☐ Not present

A flattish head is characteristic of this owl.

Bold, white 'eyebrows' give this bird its characteristically expressive face.

The neck and shoulders bear large patches of white feathers.

Underparts are pale grey-buff with prominent dark brown streaks.

Strong, sharp, curved talons hold prey securely.

In 1958 they bred in southern Scotland for the first time, although they have never managed to breed in the far north or in Ireland. In recent years, the little owl's numbers have declined in some areas but increased in others, such as the west Midlands and the south-east of England. Although the population fluctuates, it does so without any clear trend and overall seems quite stable.

Little owls can appear rather comical, which may be another reason why they became so popular as pets. When relaxed, perched on a post perhaps, the owl looks rotund and dumpy, but when alarmed or curious, it stretches up on its long legs, so it looks tall and thin, and stares with a characteristic 'surprised' or 'frowning' expression. Occasionally, the owl may turn its head upside down to get a better view of something – an ability that can be quite disconcerting to observe.

Earthworms feature heavily in the diet of little owls, and make a meal that is easy for hungry youngsters to swallow. Their predilection for ground-dwelling invertebrates means that little owls favour areas of short grassland.

The little owl is about the size of an extra-plump song thrush – substantially smaller than other British owls. It is half the size of the tawny owl. Unlike other owls, it has prominent pale 'eyebrows' above its splendid yellow eyes. Its plumage is mottled brown and cream.

Of all British owls, the little owl is the one most likely to be seen in daylight, although it prefers to hunt after dusk and before dawn. The larger short-eared owl flies in the day, too, but is much scarcer than the little owl.

Eating habits

The little owl's diet is quite different from those of the larger owls. It feeds principally on insects such as beetles, craneflies and earwigs, as well as earthworms and small rodents. Other birds are seldom eaten except during the nesting season, when the owl may take young blackbirds and house sparrows.

When hunting, the little owl usually watches for prey from a low perch, such as a fence post, dropping down with its talons spread at any sign of movement. It will also resort to running fast along the ground in pursuit of beetles or earthworms, looking rather undignified in the process.

The little owl's diet was the subject of a scientific survey by the British Trust for Ornithology from 1935 to 1937, a decade after it became well established in the wild, and this may have contributed to its survival in Britain. As this owl spread rapidly, it became the target of gamekeepers who claimed that it was a major predator of pheasant and partridge chicks.

The little owl usually nests in a tree hollow, laying eggs directly into the hole. These birds will use a nestbox, but not if it has gaps where the light can get in.

Feeding the family

Little owls hunt mainly at dusk and dawn. Most hunting is done from a perch – the owl sits motionless until it spots something in the grass below. It then leaps downward, stretching out its talons to grasp its prey. Initially, the male does most of the hunting to feed the nestlings but later the female also helps.

▲ The female owl feeds the oldest and largest chick first, sheltering it with her wing. If food is short this chick may be the only survivor. By day 16, the young weigh approximately two-thirds as much as their parent.

From its lookout post, the little owl watches for any movement on the ground below.

When potential prey is spotted, the owl leaps downward, keeping its eye on the target.

The wings are spread backwards to control the descent, and the legs and feet stretch forward in readiness.

The food is carried off in the beak to be eaten at leisure elsewhere or fed to young in the nest.

Razor-sharp talons grasp the prey as the little owl lands. Combined with the bird's weight, this kills the prey almost instantly.

However, the survey showed that although the owl did take the occasional gamebird chick, these actually formed a very small part of its diet, which was based principally on farmland pests.

Farmland is the little owl's favourite location, including cultivated fields with hedges, as well as parks and wasteland with scattered trees. It is seldom found in mountainous areas or dense woodland.

Tree-hole nests

By far the most common nest site is a hole in a deciduous tree, although suitable sites may also be found in buildings, cliffs or even rabbit burrows. Little owls also use appropriately sited nestboxes.

The male owl claims his territory early in the year and in March starts calling for a female. As she perches near the nest hole, he flies round and round her before they mate. Little owls clean out the nest hole but do not make a nest as such,

The little owl is not averse to nesting in the crevices of cliff faces. Sea cliffs, quarries and rocky ravines can all make acceptable nest sites, as long as suitable hunting grounds are to be found nearby.

LITTLE OWL CALENDAR

JANUARY ● FEBRUARY

This is often the coldest time of the year, and feeding can become difficult if the ground is frozen or covered with snow. Insects, small mammals and birds are important in the little owl's diet.

MARCH ● APRIL

Little owls are at their most vocal in early spring. Pairs call to one another and to birds in neighbouring territories. Traditional nest sites are revisited and new ones sought.

MAY ● JUNE

This is a busy time for little owl pairs, as they have eggs to incubate and then hungry chicks to feed. A constant supply of beetles, earthworms, amphibians and small mammals are caught.

JULY ● AUGUST

By midsummer, most little owl broods have fledged and left the nest. For a few weeks, the young remain in the company of their parents, relying on them for food less and less as time goes on.

SEPTEMBER ● OCTOBER

Young little owls are often forced to leave the territories of their parents and go off in search of new hunting grounds. This is a time of high mortality for the young inexperienced birds.

NOVEMBER ● DECEMBER

Autumn gales and the first frosts of winter challenge little owls, be they adults of several years or young from the previous summer. Little owls are often hit by cars at this time of year.

◄ A high proportion of the little owl's diet comprises large-bodied invertebrates, such as cockchafers and dor beetles. These pest-destroying tendencies have made the bird popular with gardeners.

► The little owl is a creature of habit, and an individual will use the same day-time roost on a regular basis, adopting a concealing upright posture.

postponed until the clutch is complete. When the young hatch, they weigh about 11g (less than half an ounce) and for the first 10 days they put on weight rapidly. Very occasionally, the male bird as well as the female participates in feeding the chicks. This is unusual among owls. Most feeding occurs from dusk to midnight, then after a gap of two hours continues until dawn. A little hunting may take place during the day.

The young leave the nest after around 30–35 days, but may return to the nest hole during the day long after this. Many die within their first few months, but if they survive beyond this they will probably go on to reach maturity at the end of one year. Individuals have been known to live for up to 17 years.

or even line the hole. Only the female incubates the eggs, although some males stay in the nest hole while she lays them. A pair will remain faithful to their territory and to each other for as long as both birds survive.

Short breeding season
The little owl lays most of its eggs between April and May, peaking at the end of April – the shortest season of any European owl. It seldom lays a second clutch, or even replaces one that has been lost. The eggs are matt white and elliptical. Incubation usually begins as soon as the first egg has been laid but, unusually for an owl, may sometimes be

Owl neighbours
Since they favour open countryside and farmland, little owls often live alongside barn owls and there appears to be little sign of conflict between the two species. This is not the case with tawny owls. Where little owls and tawny owls are found together, such as where farmland borders woodland, the little owl may be killed by its larger cousin.

Owlets are able to fly a week after leaving the nest, although their parents may continue to guard them and feed them for up to a month.

The magpie

A handsome bird of open countryside, the unmistakable magpie tends to stay near its home territory, but as the days get shorter, the birds gather in small, loose flocks, ready to converge on any food that may become available.

Bold, loud and with distinctive black-and-white plumage, the magpie is easy to recognise. A corvid, as members of the crow family are known, it has a characteristically sweeping flight but spends much of its time on the ground, its confident, high-stepping walk interspersed with a series of brisk, sideways hops and jumps.

During the 19th century, magpies were shot and trapped as vermin, and their numbers dropped to an all-time low. Since then numbers have recovered to around 650,000 pairs in Britain and 80,000 in Ireland, although there was a temporary decline in eastern Britain after the Second World War. This was linked to the use of organochlorine chemicals in farming.

▲ Magpies have a striking flight pattern. The flashing black-and-white wings and trailing black tail are instantly recognisable. The long tail and rounded wings provide agility in the air and enable the magpie to make short, rapid bursts of flight.

Population boom

Magpie numbers have increased over the last 20 or 30 years as much as threefold and this is due to several factors, many of which are related to human activities, or the lack of them. In most parts of the country, for instance, gamekeeping has declined and with fewer gamekeepers on the warpath, magpies have thrived.

The birds are exhibiting a diminishing fear of humans, too, which may help to explain their spread into suburban areas.

SUPERSTITION

Magpies are gregarious birds and are often seen in small groups. First one will appear and then another and then another. Several counting rhymes for children use magpies, including the following:

One for sorrow, two for joy,
Three for a girl and four for a boy,
Five for silver, six for gold,
Seven for a secret never to be told.

Numerous superstitions regard the magpie as a talisman of good fortune, provided that when single birds are spotted, they are always greeted or saluted in an appropriate respectful manner. Failure to do this was thought to turn the good luck into bad.

MAGPIE FACT FILE

A noisy and confident member of the crow family, the Corvidae, the magpie is an intelligent and active predator and scavenger, but in winter it eats many fruits, grains and birdtable offerings as well, especially outside the breeding season.

● **NAMES**
Common names: magpie, madge, miggy
Scientific name: *Pica pica*

● **HABITAT**
Open country and farmland with hedges and a few trees and bushes; spreading into suburban areas

● **DISTRIBUTION**
All over England, Wales, Ireland and lowland Scotland; absent from Scottish Highlands and islands

● **SIZE**
Length 44–46cm (17½–18in); weight 200–250g (7–9oz)

● **STATUS**
Threefold increase over last 30 years; up to around 650,000 pairs in Britain and 80,000 pairs in Ireland

● **KEY FEATURES**
Noisy, medium-sized with boldly pied plumage – belly white, head and wings black, iridescent (blue, green, purple and bronze) at close range; wings short, fan-like with large white panels; tail long and graduated; deep chest and short body

● **HABITS**
Sweeping flight with fluttering wingbeats alternating with brief glides; often looks weak and struggling but actually agile; high-stepping walk, sidling hops and jumps

● **VOICE**
Complex musical repertoire of several calls, including loud, harsh, quick and repeated, machine-gun like chattering, '*tchack tchack tchack …*' to signal alarm and annoyance; courtship call soft

● **FOOD**
Mainly insects in spring and summer; mostly fruit and seeds in autumn and winter; occasionally small vertebrates, including nestlings and eggs; all kinds of carrion, refuse and domestic scraps

● **BREEDING**
Peaks late April; fledge late May–June

● **NEST**
A loose, bulky structure of twigs and sticks, usually extended into roofed sphere, highly visible but vigorously defended; lined with mud, fine roots and grass; sited in crown or fork of tree or tall, often thorny shrub; often over 10m (33ft) above ground; may last for several years although new nest usually built each year, and there may be a cluster of five or six nests in the same tree

● **EGGS**
Smooth and glossy; variable in colour, generally pale green with darker markings; usually 5–8 eggs laid at daily intervals; incubation by the female lasts 17–18 days; single brood each season, but replacement clutch is laid if first fails

● **YOUNG**
Naked at hatching; brooded by female until they fledge at 22–27 days; fed by male as well after fledging; fledglings have short tails; vulnerable to crow predation

Between five and eight eggs are laid at daily intervals and hatching is staggered. If times are hard, only the older, stronger chicks will survive.

Distribution map key

▇ Present all year round

☐ Not present

The black head and chest contrast with the large white belly and wing panels.

The short, rounded wings have brilliant blue-green iridescence.

The legs are strong and quite long.

The long, graduated tail often looks wedge-shaped, and displays bronze-green iridescence, banded with reddish purple near the tip.

The magpie is adept at side-slipping, and its short, rounded wings enable it to fly at slow speeds without stalling.

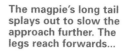

The magpie's long tail splays out to slow the approach further. The legs reach forwards...

Landing with a flourish

The magpie is skilled at handling dense tangles of trees and shrubs. Its aerial manoeuvrability is most useful when raiding the nests of smaller birds or negotiating a landing on a birdtable.

Grassland and farmland with hedges, scattered trees and bushes are the magpie's traditional habitat, but these birds are adaptable and have spread readily into towns and cities. Today there may be more magpies in some towns than on farms where hedges have been removed and old grassland ploughed.

The magpie's resurgence also owes a debt to the car. In the past, magpie numbers were probably kept in check by lack of food during the winter and early spring, but today, with an increase in the speed and amount of road traffic, so much wildlife is killed on the roads that these scavenging birds have a much

When excited, the magpie fluffs up its feathers, emphasising the white flanks and belly. A frightened bird, however, sleeks down its plumage, making itself blacker and less conspicuous.

MEAL ON THE HOOF

Along with jackdaws and starlings, magpies are often seen feeding directly off the backs of farm animals. Few host animals appear to be worried by this behaviour and they clearly benefit from the de-lousing service. The birds seek out irritating ectoparasites, such as ticks and lice, which animals such as sheep find difficult to dislodge by themselves.

For the magpie, there is another advantage in such a close association. Many birds line their nests with fur or wool. Most often this is gathered from barbed wire, thorns, the ground or dead animals. However, occasionally a cheeky magpie will tweak the wool directly from the sheep's back to take back to its nest.

The bird takes only loose wool – no matter how amicable the relationship between bird and mammal, attempting to pluck out firmly attached wool would be going too far – and only a small amount of wool is needed for the nest, so this is not a serious loss for either the sheep or the farmer.

▼ Magpies are so bold they may feed off live hosts such as sheep, providing them with welcome relief. Ticks found in the animal's coat are a good source of nourishment for birds. The grey, pea-sized parasite, bloated with blood, makes an ideal beakful for magpies.

improved chance of surviving the months of hardship. Other scavenging corvids, such as crows and jackdaws, have shown a similar rise in numbers.

Magpies and songbirds

Magpies have been accused of reducing the numbers of small songbirds by stealing eggs and even small chicks. Although these do form a natural component of the magpie's diet, there is no evidence that magpies have caused any long-term damage. After all, they have co-evolved with all the other native bird species over millions of years.

...and another perfect landing is accomplished. The magpie folds its wings and balances using its tail as a counterweight.

Magpies favour prominent perches as lookout posts. Watching the world from this privileged viewpoint ensures they are often first to spot a potential feast.

Although magpies have been seen attacking robins, blackbirds and song thrushes in suburban gardens – and sometimes it may appear that no young songbirds are allowed to fledge at all – detailed research has demonstrated that the decline in numbers of small bird species, including the bullfinch, linnet, skylark, song thrush, tree sparrow and reed bunting, is due to a variety of other factors, especially modern farming and gardening practices as well as habitat loss. Magpies are certainly not the cause of their demise except on a very local and temporary level. Indeed, various surveys have shown that where magpies are thriving, so are songbirds, because they benefit from the same conditions.

Magpies do take eggs and nestlings, however, especially when they are nesting themselves. Nests are searched for in a systematic way and an entire clutch of possibly five baby blackbirds may be taken over a period of just a couple of hours. Songbirds are resilient creatures, though, and are likely to succeed with another brood. They have evolved to cope with high mortality among their young due to cold weather, lack of food, and a variety of predators, including magpies.

Team effort

Magpies will collaborate when hunting. Pairs can often be seen working together along hedgerows or woodland edges, trying to find occupied nests of small birds, and steadfastly refusing to be deterred by the angry cries of the parent birds. The magpies' technique demonstrates real cooperation between the pair, with one of the birds searching close to the cover and the other keeping a short distance away so that it can detect any birds that are successfully flushed out.

▲ Like other corvids, magpies are efficient scavengers, forever on the lookout for an easy meal, such as this dead mouse. They perform a beneficial function by removing carrion quickly from the countryside.

◀ A magpie will rob another bird's nest if it gets the chance. Nests built in exposed locations, such as sparse hedgerows or garden shrubberies, are the most vulnerable to predation.

In early spring magpies gather with the aim of acquiring a territory or finding a mate. At this time individuals preen themselves often, making their plumage look as impressive as possible.

A magpie feeding habit more often associated with the jay is the collection of acorns in autumn. Magpies collect and store these nutritious nuts for food later in the winter. Jays may cover several miles to reach a good oak tree, but magpies tend to use trees that happen to be within their territories.

Social behaviour

The ultimate goal of every magpie is to become a member of an established pair with a good breeding territory. To achieve this, both males and females must establish their credentials among other magpies in the neighbourhood. A magpie higher in the social order may puff out its plumage to display as much of the white as possible while slightly fanning its secondary feathers, effectively emphasising the pale feathers. Birds lower in the social order sleek down their feathers to make themselves look mainly black.

Magpies without territories congregate in loose flocks, where the social hierarchy, or pecking order, is established through similar social interactions between the birds. Sometimes clashes ensue – these usually amount to no more than aggressive posturing, but occasionally real violence erupts.

This gathering of birds in non-breeding flocks normally peaks in midwinter. The birds may not stay together all of the time, but if any one of them finds a good source of food – where cattle or other livestock are being fed, for instance – as many as 15, 20 or even 30 birds may converge.

In spring, such gatherings provide the opportunity for any unpaired birds to compete for a territory and establish a pair bond through mutual displaying. Magpie displays incorporate wing and tail flicks, sometimes accompanied by a soft warbling song from the male.

MAGPIE CALENDAR

JANUARY • FEBRUARY

Territorial pairs begin to build their nests in January, an endeavour that may take them some time – up to eight weeks. Pairs forcibly exclude other magpies from their own patch.

MARCH • APRIL

The egg-laying period usually reaches a peak around April. Magpies are not immune to nest predation and sometimes must defend their nests vociferously from the attentions of crows or squirrels.

MAY • JUNE

Predation on the nests of small birds peaks when the magpies have their own young to feed in May. The youngsters fledge at the end of the month but stay with their parents for another six weeks.

JULY • AUGUST

The short-tailed young birds become independent and begin to disperse. This may simply mean short trips of a few hundred yards in a good area, or several miles in areas that can support few birds.

SEPTEMBER • OCTOBER

Territories are re-established in earnest. Many sites will be occupied by a pair of adult birds, but others will contain quite large numbers of unpaired birds that join together in loose flocks.

NOVEMBER • DECEMBER

During cold periods with food shortages, carrion – often road casualties – forms an important part of the magpie's diet. Birds will feed on even very busy roads by scavenging early in the morning.

◄ On sunny days, a magpie will position itself so that the warmth of the sun can reach its skin. The bird fluffs out its feathers and holds its wings downwards so that as much of its body is exposed as possible. Sunning is usually followed by a bout of vigorous preening.

▼ The magpie's iridescent plumage must be kept clean and in good condition at all times, so birds are frequently seen bathing in shallow pools and then preening nearby.

Health concerns

In recent years, it has come to the attention of some health authorities that a number of people were suffering from a gastric disease caused by *Campylobacter* bacteria (often found in the stomachs of hedgehogs). Sufferers were clustered in distinct areas and detective work narrowed down the common factor to people who had milk delivered to their doorstep. Doorstep watches revealed that magpies were piercing the metallic tops and inserting their beaks into the bottle neck to feed on the milk. The magpies, which may have been scavenging dead animals immediately beforehand, were believed to have transferred the disease organism to the milk.

Magpies have also discovered that egg cartons contain eggs and have been known to use their sharp bills to penetrate the boxes and shells. They have even been recorded entering dairy warehouses to steal the milk.

Magpies and man

Adaptable and intelligent, magpies are easy to tame, and rescued birds can live much longer in captivity than those in the wild. One in 100 wild fledglings may live for as long as six or seven years, but a bird looked after well in captivity might survive for a decade or more.

However, once a wild magpie has become tame it cannot be returned to the wild because it will have learned to be friendly towards humans. Attempting to land on the shoulder of an unwary pedestrian, for instance, may easily be interpreted as an attack. Be careful of taking an adandoned chick or injured bird into the house. Caring for either is best left to an expert from the RSPB.

The magpie's nest is a bulky construction of twigs and sticks that is often extended to form a domed ball. The female sits on her high nest, which is not well concealed, for up to three weeks, guarding the eggs and chicks against marauding crows.

PROTECTING SONGBIRDS

Although it is impossible to stop magpies from feeding on the eggs and chicks of other, smaller birds, there are things that people can do to increase the survival of small songbirds. The most important factor is the provision of good habitat. If gardens provide varied sites in which birds can nest, some, at least, are likely to be successful.

People with gardens that are too small for this strategy to be practical should instead encourage small birds to nest in places that are not vulnerable to magpies. For instance, leaving a shed window slightly ajar will allow little birds to nest inside while excluding the larger magpies.

Vulnerable open nests can be protected with an enveloping ball of wire netting, the mesh size of which will let in the nesting bird but not the magpie – holes of 5–8cm (2–3in) are probably sufficient. However, be careful not to touch the nest itself or the eggs inside.

Spinners of silk

**Spiders are well known for weaving beautiful, intricate webs
out of silken threads, but they are not the only creatures to make use
of this immensely strong and versatile material.**

**Shimmering with dew or highlighted
by hoarfrost, orb webs are an
unmissable feature of early autumn
mornings. Each spider often weaves a
new web within the outer framework
every day at around dawn or at night.**

From the moment a spider hatches
out of the egg, it embarks on a
lifetime of almost continuous silk
production. Every spider spins several
kinds of silk, each one produced by a
separate specialised gland in its abdomen.
The silk is put to a great variety of uses –
as a thread for the spider to travel down,
for wrapping prey and for covering eggs,
as well as for constructing webs.

Spinning silk is a complicated business,
but the techniques are all innate in
spiders. They instinctively know when
to spin each kind of silk, and each gland
has its own ducts leading to the outside
of the body.

Usually, three pairs of spinnerets, from
which the silk is extruded, are to be
found at the rear of the body. In some
species, including the house spider, these
look like tiny, flexible 'fingers', but in
others they are small and hardly visible.
Silk emerges through tiny tubes and
pores (called spigots) on the tips of the
spinnerets. Blood pressure triggers the
initial flow of silk, but the glands are not

Making an orb web

*The familiar wheel-shaped orb webs are
perfectly designed for catching flying
insects. Construction techniques may
vary between species and the position
of the web, but all orb web spiders
follow a basic plan.*

**First, the spider links two suitable
anchor points with a bridge thread,
then pulls the thread taut. A slack
thread is trailed below the bridge, from
which the spider drops on a lifeline,
which it anchors to a fixed point below.**

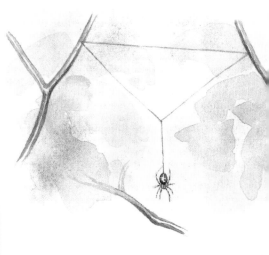

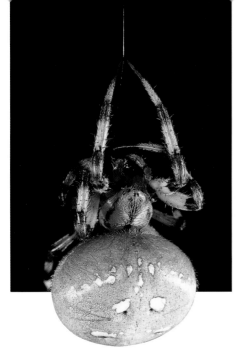

▲ Spider's silk is very strong. Just a single thin thread, extruded from the abdomen, supports the weight of this female four-spotted orb spider, *Araneus quadratus*, even though her body is bloated with eggs.

This grasshopper has taken its last leap – straight into the sticky web of a female garden spider (*Araneus diadenatus*). To make doubly sure that escape is impossible, the spider wraps her prey in a shroud of silk.

equipped with muscles to pump it out. Instead, the silken thread has to be drawn out and manipulated by the spider's legs.

Orb webs

The wheel-shaped webs commonly seen in Britain belong to orb web spiders, of which there are approximately 40 species, typified by the garden spider. The complex web is constructed around a simple 'Y' frame. The basic framework is spun with non-sticky silk before the spiral threads are replaced with sticky ones that will entrap the spider's prey.

The gum that coats the threads is produced by another gland in the spider's abdomen. This substance breaks into droplets as the silk is stretched out, and it is on these droplets that dew condenses to give the wonderful jewel-like effect that can be seen on early mornings. The gum is very sticky but the spider avoids getting caught up in its own web by coating its feet with an oily substance produced by yet another gland.

Using its legs as rulers, the spider ensures that each sticky thread is exactly the right distance from the next – threads that are too close together would be a waste of silk and threads that are too far apart would let prey slip through. The silken threads are very strong, so when the spider needs to sever or adjust the length of a strand it does not cut it with its jaws. Instead, it drips digestive juices on to the thread from its mouthparts, dissolving it away. The spider works fast and efficiently and can build an orb web from scratch in less than an hour.

Webs are regularly rebuilt because even if they are not damaged by prey, the sticky threads are rendered ineffective by rain and dust in the air. The old silk is eaten by the spider and quickly recycled.

SILKEN THREAD

Silk is a complex protein produced in various glands. Its exact composition varies from species to species and also according to its function. Nevertheless, silk from a silkworm or any other caterpillar is fundamentally the same as spider silk.

Although initially secreted in a liquid form, the spider's silk solidifies and hardens as soon as it emerges from the body. This change is due to the stretching of the silk as it is pulled from the body. Stretching changes the orientation of the silk molecules, causing them to line up in long chains.

Spider silk is one of the strongest and most stretchy materials known. It is stronger than steel wire of the same thickness and is amazingly elastic. Some silks can be stretched to more than twice their original length before they snap.

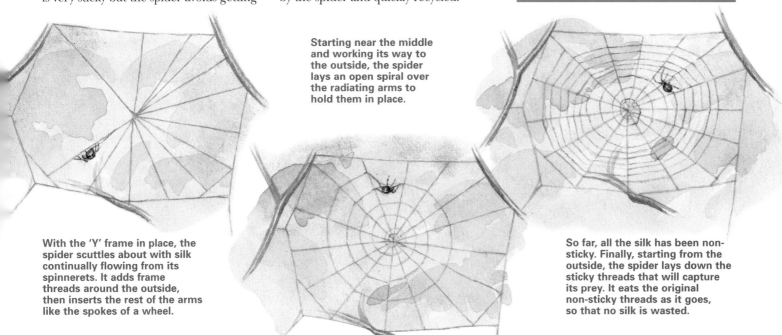

With the 'Y' frame in place, the spider scuttles about with silk continually flowing from its spinnerets. It adds frame threads around the outside, then inserts the rest of the arms like the spokes of a wheel.

Starting near the middle and working its way to the outside, the spider lays an open spiral over the radiating arms to hold them in place.

So far, all the silk has been non-sticky. Finally, starting from the outside, the spider lays down the sticky threads that will capture its prey. It eats the original non-sticky threads as it goes, so that no silk is wasted.

Types of web

Spiders are a large and diverse group of creatures. Every species makes its own distinctive web, each designed to catch prey in a subtly different way.

The webs of *Amaurobius* are often seen coating tree bark. These collars of bluish silk are adapted to catch insects that crawl over the surface.

The haphazard webs of *Theridion sisyphium* are used to catch flying insects. They are invariably located next to silken retreats, in which the spiders hide.

The hammock webs of linyphiid spiders consist of a horizontal or slightly domed silken sheet. This tends to sag like a hammock when covered with dew.

The webs of house spiders are delicate sheets, usually found in the corner of a room or on a windowsill, where they collect dust as well as catching insects and other spiders.

► In deciduous woodland in spring, armies of small caterpillars descend from the tree canopy on silken strands in search of fresh food or a place to pupate.

When an insect becomes ensnared by the web, the spider brings yet another silk gland into play. This gland produces a broad band of silk, composed of many fine strands. The spider fixes the silk to its prey, which it then rotates using its legs. More and more silk is drawn out of the spider's body until the prey is well and truly wrapped. This package is then stored to be eaten at the spider's leisure.

Hammock webs
The orb web is just one of many different kinds of web, not all of which are actually sticky. Hammock webs, which clothe rough grass and other vegetation in the autumn, are the work of money spiders and other members of the family Linyphiidae. These account for about 40 per cent of all British spiders.

Each web consists of a horizontal or slightly domed silk sheet, which tends to sag like a hammock when covered with dew. Planthoppers and other small insects that land on the sheet get their feet tangled in the fabric and are unable to escape before the spider grabs them from below. Many spiders spin a three-dimensional trellis of tripwires above their hammock webs, which sends small flying insects crashing onto the sheet.

Sticky traps
Scruffy, lace-like webs on old walls and fences are the work of spiders of the *Amaurobius* species. The webs tend to cling to your fingers but the stickiness is not caused by glue. These spiders spin the finest of all silks – about 0.000015mm in diameter. The spider extrudes a band of silk, consisting of many of these gossamer threads, from a finely

perforated plate called the cribellum. It combs out the silk using bristles on each back leg. Rapid vibration of the spider's legs then throws the threads into microscopic loops. The finished product acts like Velcro, trapping the feet, bristles or spines of any insect that comes into contact with it.

Caterpillar silk
All caterpillars produce silk. For some it may only provide an anchorage while they change their skins, but other caterpillars spend most of their lives hidden under protective tents of silk. Many escape from predators by lowering themselves on silken lifelines. The most familiar use of silk by caterpillars is to build the cocoons in which they will later pupate, although not all caterpillars make cocoons.

Caterpillars produce their silk in modified salivary glands, which open through a pore or spinneret on the lower jaw. When a caterpillar is ready to pupate, it selects a suitable spot, often clinging to a twig or nestling in a cluster of leaves, and settles down to hours or even days of spinning. Dabbing its jaw down to attach the still sticky silk to the surroundings, it

Eggar moth caterpillars live in a roughly spherical web of woven silk that they produce themselves. The web serves as a safe retreat during the day, the caterpillars emerging at night to feed.

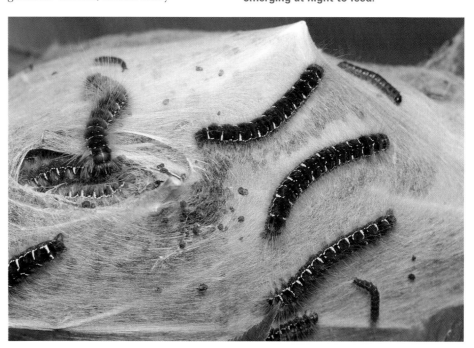

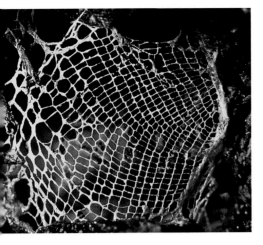

Some types of caddis fly larvae, which live in flowing water, use silk to build a web-like construction. Slung between submerged plants, the net traps any food items that may be brought along by the current.

Most caterpillars produce numerous, relatively short strands of silk, which are not suitable for commercial use. The world's silk supplies come mainly from the caterpillar of the silk moth, *Bombyx mori*, which has been farmed in its native China for nearly 5000 years. Its high-quality silk is produced in a single long unbroken strand – sometimes there is as much as a kilometre (around two-thirds of a mile) of silk in a single cocoon. The silk moth has been bred in captivity for so long that it no longer survives in the wild.

▶ Silk moth caterpillars spin their silk cocoons as a safe refuge while they pupate. These adult moths are newly emerged from the cocoons.

then lifts its head to draw out the first strand of silk. Round and round the head spins, and by twisting its body this way and that the caterpillar gradually swathes itself in silken strands. Inside this flimsy shelter, it continues to turn and spin until it is completely enclosed in a cocoon.

Other spinners

The larvae of many other insects pupate in silken cocoons, including those of fleas, some flies, sawflies, a number of ants and lacewings. The latter are unusual in that the silk is produced in modified excretory organs and secreted through the anus.

Skipper butterflies pupate in flimsy cocoons. The ringlet and a few other brown butterflies also pupate under a few strands of silk, but most butterfly pupae (or chrysalids) are naked, attached by their rear ends to little pads of silk that the caterpillars have spun on convenient supports. Some hang from the pads, while others are held upright by silken girdles.

Caddis fly larvae are best known for their portable homes or cases, which are essentially silk body stockings to which the insects attach debris. As the insect grows, it adds new collars of silk, which it decorates to act as camouflage. Caddis silk is secreted by modified salivary glands, like those of caterpillars.

Sometimes silk is produced purely to give away. The dance fly, *Hilara maura* – a little black fly most often seen in fast-moving 'dancing' swarms over ponds and streams – is one of many species where the male uses silk to prepare an offering for his mate. The male catches another tiny insect, wraps it in a bag of shiny silk, manufactured in glands in his swollen front legs, and offers it to the female. The gift probably encourages her to mate but it is not always eaten. In fact, the females often drop the gifts, and the males can sometimes get away with presenting potential mates with empty silk balloons.

Silk nuisance

For gardeners the sight of silk on their plants can sometimes indicate an infestation of unwanted pests. The various kinds of red spider mites that damage fruit trees and other cultivated plants trail silk wherever they go. Stems and leaves are coated with mats and ropes of silk that literally drip from the plants when an infestation is heavy.

By late summer, spiders are very common in the countryside. However, the scale of their numbers is often not fully appreciated until the first misty mornings of autumn highlight the gossamer threads of silk.

WILDLIFE WATCH

Where can I see webs and other examples of silk?

● Grassland, woods and hedges are the places to look for spiders' webs. In early autumn, spiders are at their most numerous and their webs are often highlighted by dew drops and hence easy to see.

● Visit an oak woodland in May or June to see roller moth caterpillars abseiling to the ground. Early mornings are best, as the silk strands are highlighted by shafts of sunlight.

● If you find an orb web in summer with a large female spider resting in it, watch quietly for a few minutes and you may see a tiny male approaching. The suitor tentatively signals his intentions to the female by tapping the silk in order to avoid being mistaken for a potential meal. Despite this precaution, many male spiders are eaten by their partners after mating.

● To see silk worms feeding on mulberry leaves and the reeling of silk threads from cocoons, visit Lullingstone Silk Farm in Dorset (telephone 01935 474608).

● To see caterpillars as well as spiders, visit The Butterfly Farm, Swan's Nest Lane, Stratford-upon-Avon, Warwickshire (telephone 01789 299288, or visit www.butterflyfarm.co.uk).

The harvestmen

Distant relatives of spiders and mites, harvestmen emerge at dusk to clamber through the grass in search of insects to eat. Sensitive tips on their long spindly legs help to pinpoint the prey.

Often thought to be spiders, since they share their eight-legged body form, harvestmen are actually very different creatures. Unlike spiders they cannot produce silk to make webs, and they do not have venomous fangs. So although both spiders and harvestmen are arachnids – along with scorpions, ticks and mites – they are classified separately. Spiders belong to the order Araneae, and harvestmen to the Opiliones.

Pea-like bodies
The most obvious difference between them is that a spider's body has two distinct parts. The front half, to which the legs are attached, is the prosoma or cephalothorax, and the rear half is the opisthosoma or abdomen. The two parts are separated by a distinct waist. A harvestman's body consists of the same two parts, but since there is no more than a shallow groove between them, they appear to form a single unit.

The most familiar harvestmen have very long legs, up to 30 times the length of their bodies. However, many harvestmen that live on the ground have legs that are barely longer than their bodies. In all species the second pair of legs is always the longest. These are packed with nerves and sensory cells, and are the animal's primary sense organs. A harvestman depends on these legs to find food. It keeps all its legs clean by washing them regularly and fastidiously, which it

▲ A close-up view of *Leiobunum rotundum* shows its apparently one-piece body, central eye-turret and chelicerae. This individual has lost one of its extra-long, sensory second pair of legs, which will reduce its chances of long-term survival.

does by drawing them gracefully through its mouthparts to remove every tiny particle of food or dirt.

A harvestman has just two eyes, unlike spiders which have six or eight, and these are carried on a little turret on top of the body called an ocularium. They are not very efficient and probably do little more than detect whether it is day or night. A harvestman also has a pair of leg-like sensory projections called pedipalps at the front of its body, which act rather like antennae. Right at the front, hidden by the pedipalps, are a pair of tiny jaw-like horns, or chelicerae. These are equivalent to the fangs of a spider, although they have no venom. The harvestman uses them like forceps to cut and tear up food.

Nocturnal foragers
Harvestmen are mainly active at night when the air is moist. They are essentially carnivores, eating carrion as well as living prey. Insects, spiders, woodlice and other harvestmen all figure in their diet. Some of the ground-living species, such as *Trogulus tricarinatus*, eat a lot of snails.

The long legs of many harvestmen enable them to crawl through foliage with surprising speed. Most species are more active after dark, but they can also be seen on the move in the morning and evening.

A *Phalangium opilio* harvestman walks among grass stems. Its progress is leisurely, but if disturbed by vibrations, it changes gear and scuttles off into the undergrowth.

When a harvestman detects prey with the sensitive tips of its second pair of legs, it drops on to the prey, pins it to the ground, and tears it to pieces with its mouthparts. The bases of the pedipalps help to crush the prey and cut it up, so the animal can suck the resulting small particles into its mouth. Harvestmen also eat fungi and fallen fruit, as well as bird droppings and other dung in small quantities. They cannot survive for more than a few days without water, and drink regularly from dew or moist ground.

While hunting they are at risk from predators, but they are protected by pungent secretions emitted by glands near the bases of their front legs. These are not perceptible to humans but they certainly deter ants and many spiders, which will promptly cut trapped harvestmen out of their webs. Despite this they have many enemies, including frogs, toads, small mammals and many birds.

Quick workers
Males and females are much alike, although the females are often slightly bigger. They have no courtship and when they bump into each other they simply grip each other's pedipalps to get into a face-to-face position, allowing the male to slide his very long, slender penis below the female and inject sperm into her

DID YOU KNOW?
If grabbed by a predator, a harvestman can escape by shedding one of its legs. The severed limb continues to twitch for up to an hour, distracting the predator for long enough for the harvestman to escape. Although it cannot regenerate the lost leg, it can manage perfectly well with less than a full set. However, if the insect loses one of the second, sensory pair, it is at a serious disadvantage, since it will be harder to find food.

body. Mating is usually over within seconds but harvestmen often mate several times in succession, with the same or any other available individuals. Parthenogenesis – or virgin birth – occurs in some species, such as *Megabunus diadema*, where females outnumber males by up to 100 to one.

The female uses her long ovipositor – a tube projecting from the rear of her body – to lay eggs in small batches in soil or debris. Most species lay their eggs in the autumn and these remain in the ground until the spring. Some lay their eggs in early summer. The young are nearly fully grown by the autumn when they become dormant, completing their development the following spring. Young harvestmen are miniature replicas of their parents, and mature in two or three months, after several skin changes. They usually die after laying their own eggs.

Varied habitats
The 24 species of British harvestmen can be grouped by their habitats. Most of them occur in either leaf litter, low-growing vegetation or trees and bushes, and some may live in or near houses.

Nemastoma bimaculatum is common in leaf litter. It can be recognised by its long legs and the two white spots on its dark body. Another leaf-litter species is *Homalenotus quadridentatus*, identified by the four 'teeth' at the rear of its body.

Low-growing vegetation supports many species, mostly with medium-length legs. *Paroligolophus agrestis* is abundant here. It

varies from silvery grey to pinkish brown and usually has a pale stripe along the centre of its back. *Mitopus morio* is also common, with a black saddle that comes to a point near the rear of its body. *Oligolophus tridens* can be distinguished by three upward-pointing spines on the front edge of the cephalothorax. The underside of *Phalangium opilio* is very pale but its upper surface is dotted with short, black-tipped spines.

Some of the longest-legged harvestmen live in trees and bushes. None has longer legs than *Leiobunum rotundum*, which is also common in gardens. *Megabunus diadema* may be recognised by the long spines on its eye-turret. Several species are associated with gardens, including *Odiellus spinosus*, the bulkiest British harvestman, and *Opilio parietinus*, which is easily identified by its spotted underside.

▲ During the day harvestmen avoid activity, congregating in large groups to hide or bask in the sun. Their long legs form a living mesh that makes one individual almost indistinguishable from another.

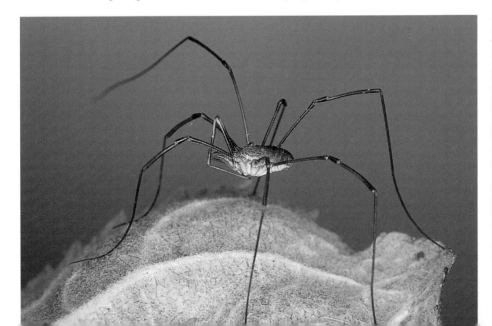

◀ A front view of a male *Phalangium opilio* harvestman shows the chelicerae at the front of the body, which are used to tear up insects and other items of food.

WILDLIFE WATCH

How can I find harvestmen?

● Quietly probe rough grass and other vegetation to find harvestmen, using your fingers or a pencil or some other small implement. Another way is carefully to sweep through some lush vegetation with a sturdy net to see what you can catch.

● Put some heaps of leaf litter on a sheet of white paper and gently search through it to see what it contains.

Wild berries

Hedgerows laden with ripening blackberries are a common sight in autumn. The rose family, to which such berries belong, also includes many other fruiting plants, from agrimony to meadowsweet.

The rose family, Rosaceae, is a large and conspicuous group of native plants. As well as the wild roses, this amazingly varied family includes meadowsweet and its allies, plants with fleshy fruits (called drupes) such as blackberry and strawberry, and the avens and agrimonies with their dry hooked or plumed fruits (called achenes).

These plants are all perennials or shrubs. Several have vigorous structures for reproduction, such as the runners of strawberry, the creeping rhizomes or thickened underground stems of raspberry and cloudberry, and the rooting, arched shoots of blackberry.

Varied leaves and fruits

Rose leaves may be undivided, three to five-lobed or, more commonly, compound with one to six or more pairs of leaflets. These are toothed and often unequal in size, with the end leaflet being considerably larger. At the base of each leaf stalk is a pair of small, leafy flanges called stipules. The flowers have a fleshy basal part, which often enlarges when in fruit. Most have five sepals and five white, yellow or pinkish petals – mountain avens is the exception with eight petals – and numerous stamens and ovules, which develop into many small fruits.

Individual fruits usually contain one seed and are clustered into tight heads or 'berries'. Bridewort has clusters of dry, several-seeded fruits or follicles that split when ripe. Meadowsweet and dropwort have dry, one-seeded fruits, as does strawberry – in this case, the tiny fruits are arranged on the surface of the fleshy, red swollen base of the flower. The strawberry itself is not a true fruit.

Blackberry and raspberry have clusters of small, one-seeded, fleshy drupelets that make up the fruit. Here the swollen base of the flower forms a cone-like central axis, which remains after the fruit is gone. The sweet flesh of the drupes makes them a popular food for small mammals and birds, which disperse the seeds via their droppings.

The avens employ a different method of dispersal. They produce round heads of dry, one-seeded fruits, each

▲ Blackberries are still gathered from the wild. The differences in varieties mean that fruiting times vary slightly, even along a single stretch of hedgerow.

with a thickened, stalked hook that is derived from the stigma. The ripe heads break up easily and the hooks attach themselves firmly to the fur of passing animals – or people's socks – so carrying the seeds far and wide.

The fruits of mountain avens have plumed stigmas and are dispersed by the wind. In pirri-pirri-bur, clinging red bristles come from the base of the flower. Agrimony has one to two fruits contained within the enlarged flower-base. The outside of this dispersal unit is armed with Velcro-like whorls of hooked bristles.

◄ Jam made from the fruits of cloudberry is popular in Scandinavia. Cloudberry rarely fruits in Britain because of a scarcity of female plants.

Bramble or blackberry
Rubus fruticosus agg.

Stone bramble
Rubus saxatilis

Raspberry
Rubus idaeus

Cloudberry
Rubus chamaemorus

Dewberry
Rubus caesius

WILD BERRIES FACT FILE

● **Bramble or blackberry**
Rubus fruticosus agg.
Habitat and distribution
Abundant and invasive in woods, scrub, hedges, heathland, wasteground and untended gardens
Size Stems up to 4m (13ft) long
Key features
A robust, shrubby perennial, forming tangles of arched or sprawling, ridged, fiercely prickly stems; leaves with 3–5 oval, toothed leaflets prickly beneath; flowers white or pink, 20–32mm (¾–1¼in) across, often in large clusters; fruit purplish black, shiny, with numerous drupelets
Flowering time
May–November

● **Stone bramble**
Rubus saxatilis
Habitat and distribution
Scattered in rocky woods and shady screes, mostly in northern Britain, Wales, and northern and western Ireland
Size Stems up to 40cm (15¾in) long
Key features
A tufted perennial with branched, leafy, prickly stems; leaves with 3 oval, toothed leaflets; flowers dull white, 8–15mm (⅜–⅝in) across, in loose clusters of 3–10; fruit scarlet with 2–6 drupelets
Flowering time
June–August

● **Raspberry**
Rubus idaeus
Habitat and distribution
Widespread in woods, scrub, damp heaths and on mountains
Size Up to 2m (6½ft) tall
Key features
A perennial, forming thickets of erect, slightly prickly stems; leaves with 3–5 oval, toothed leaflets that are downy white beneath; flowers dull white or pinkish, about 10mm (⅜in) across, in small, loose clusters; fruit a small, red berry with numerous drupelets
Flowering time
May–August

● **Cloudberry**
Rubus chamaemorus
Habitat and distribution
Widespread on peaty heather moors in northern Britain, Snowdonia, North Wales and north-west Ireland
Size Up to 20cm (8in) tall
Key features
A low-growing perennial; 1–3 leaves, with 5–7 blunt lobes; flowers white, solitary, 25–40mm (1–1⅝in) across, not appearing every year; fruit red then orange, resembles a raspberry but has fewer, larger drupelets
Flowering time
June–July

● **Dewberry**
Rubus caesius
Habitat and distribution
Widespread in open woods, scrub, rough grassland and sand dunes; rarer in Scotland and Ireland
Size Stems up to 4m (13ft) long
Key features
Similar to blackberry but less robust and prickly; stems slender, unridged, greyish when young; leaves with 3 leaflets; flowers white 20–25mm (¾–1in) across; fruits with greyish bloom and few, large drupelets
Flowering time
May–September

No one knows for certain how the name raspberry originated. One theory is that the berries were used to make a wine that resembled *vin rapé* or 'rasped wine'.

ROSE RELATIVES FACT FILE

● **Wild strawberry**
Fragaria vesca
Habitat and distribution
Common in open woods, on sunny banks and heaths and open, stony wasteground
Size Up to 30cm (1ft) tall
Key features
A low-growing, tufted, hairy perennial, forming extensive patches by far-creeping, reddish runners; leaves bright green above, pale and silky-haired beneath, with 3 oval, toothed leaflets; flowers white, on drooping stalks, 12–18mm (½–¾in) across, in small clusters; fruit a tiny, globular strawberry
Flowering time
May–July

● **Herb bennet or wood avens**
Geum urbanum
Habitat and distribution
Common in open woods, woodland rides, hedgebanks and shady gardens
Size Up to 70cm (2ft 4in) tall
Key features
An erect, branched, leafy, hairy perennial; leaves with 1–5 pairs of unequal leaflets; flowers yellow, star-shaped, 8–15mm (⅜–⅝in) across, in very loose clusters; round cluster of hooked, bronze-tipped, 1-seeded fruits
Flowering time
May–November (later in mild winters)

● **Water avens**
Geum rivale
Habitat and distribution
Widespread in damp or shady places and hedgerows in northern and western Britain; scarcer in south and in Ireland
Size Up to 50cm (20in) tall
Key features
Similar to wood avens, but leaves with 3–6 pairs of leaflets; flowers pinkish purple with notched petals, darker purplish sepals, bell-shaped, nodding, 10–18mm (⅜–¾in) long
Flowering time
April–September

● **Mountain avens**
Dryas octopetala
Habitat and distribution
Cliffs, screes and rocky grassland on limestone, mainly upland; rare but abundant in places, especially in western Ireland and north-western Scotland
Size Stems up to 50cm (20in) long
Key features
A mat-forming shrublet with branched, woody creeping stems; leaves dark green on upper surface, densely downy white beneath, toothed, almost oblong; flowers white with large central cluster of golden yellow stamens, solitary, dish-shaped, 25–35mm (1–1⅜in) across; produces a cluster of feathery, 1-seeded fruits, twisted at the top
Flowering time
May–August

● **Agrimony**
Agrimonia eupatoria
Habitat and distribution
Common in open woods, scrub, hedges and rough grassland; rare in northern Scotland
Size Up to 1m (3ft) tall
Key features
An erect, leafy perennial; leaves whitish beneath, with 3–6 pairs of large leaflets and smaller leaflets between; flowers yellow, star-shaped, 5–8mm (¼–⅜in) across, in a long spike; fruit inverted cone-shaped, grooved, with erect or spreading bristles at the top
Flowering time
June–September

● **Fragrant agrimony**
Agrimonia procera
Habitat and distribution
Scattered in similar habitats to agrimony, but usually on more lime-poor soils, north to central Scotland
Size Up to 1.5m (5ft) tall
Key features
Similar to agrimony but more robust, the leaves more abundant, deeply toothed and fragrant, green with sticky hairs beneath, with downturned bristles at the top of less furrowed fruits
Flowering time
June–August

● **Bastard agrimony**
Aremonia agrimonioides
Habitat and distribution
Originally from central Europe, naturalised in a few woods in Perthshire and elsewhere
Size Up to 35cm (14in) tall
Key features
Similar to agrimony but much smaller, leaves with 3–5 pairs of very unequal leaflets; few inconspicuous yellow flowers in branched clusters; fruit rounded without bristles
Flowering time
June–July

Water avens
Geum rivale

Herb bennet or wood avens
Geum urbanum

Wild strawberry
Fragaria vesca

Mountain avens is a mat-forming plant that is confined to rock ledges in mountainous areas in the north and west. Feathery, twisted seed heads develop after the large white flowers have finished.

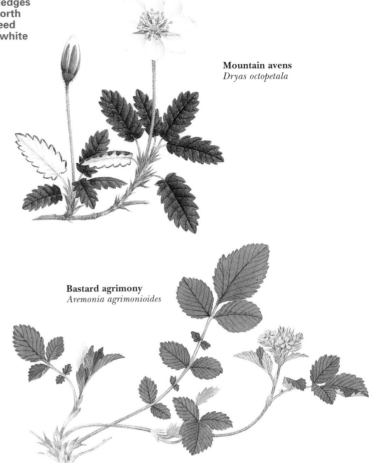

Mountain avens
Dryas octopetala

Bastard agrimony
Aremonia agrimonioides

Fragrant agrimony
Agrimonia procera

Agrimony
Agrimonia eupatoria

Although few people still gather the fruits of the wild strawberry, they are far superior in flavour to the larger, cultivated varieties. The plant is quite common in open woodland and scrub.

ROSE RELATIVES FACT FILE

● **Meadowsweet**
Filipendula ulmaria
Habitat and distribution
Common in marshes, fens, ditches, damp fields and woods
Size Up to 2m (6½ft) tall
Key features
A robust, hairy perennial with leafy stems; basal leaves with up to 5 pairs of large leaflets and smaller leaflets between; flowers 4–8mm (⅛–⅜in) across, pale cream, sweet-scented, in dense, frothy mass; 1-seeded fruits joined in twisted clusters
Flowering time
June–September

● **Dropwort**
Filipendula vulgaris
Habitat and distribution
Grassland on chalk and limestone from Devon to the Scottish border; in Ireland only in the Burren
Size Up to 70cm (2ft 4in) tall
Key features
Similar to meadowsweet; basal leaves with 8 or more pairs of large leaflets; petals tinged pinkish in bud, unscented flowers 8–16mm (¼–¾in) across; fruit cluster twisted
Flowering time
May–August

● **Bridewort or willow spiraea**
Spiraea x pseudosalicifolia
Habitat and distribution
Planted or naturalised in hedges and on railway embankments
Size Up to 2m (6½ft) tall
Key features
An erect, branched shrub; leaves 4–8cm (1½–3in) long, almost stalkless, elliptical, upper ones saw-toothed; flowers pink, in dense, almost cylindrical clusters up to 12cm (4¾in) long; fruit a cluster of 5 pods
Flowering time
June–September

● **Pirri-pirri-bur**
Acaena novae-zelandiae
Habitat and distribution:
Originally from New Zealand, established on a few heaths, hedgebanks and sand dunes
Size Stems up to 20cm (8in) long
Key features
A creeping perennial, forming extensive patches; leaves with 3–5 pairs of unequal, toothed leaflets; flowers without petals but each with 4 pale green sepals, in dense, globular clusters, about 10mm (⅜in) across, on long stalks; round, long red-bristled cluster of 1-seeded fruits, soon breaking apart
Flowering time
June–July

Meadowsweet
Filipendula ulmaria

Dropwort
Filipendula vulgaris

Pirri-pirri-bur
Acaena novae-zelandiae

WILDLIFE WATCH

Where can I see rose relatives?

● Most of the fruiting roses are widespread on waysides, in hedgerows and along woodland margins. They even occur as garden weeds. Meadowsweet grows in damp fields and woodland rides, while the much scarcer dropwort favours grassland on chalk or limestone.

● Mountain avens is particularly common in parts of northern Britain and the Burren of County Clare in Ireland. Cloudberry is widespread in the Highlands of Scotland.

Bridewort or willow spiraea
Spiraea x pseudosalicifolia

The frothy cream flowers of meadowsweet decorate riverside meadows and brim from damp ditches throughout Britain in July, filling the air with their powerful scent.

Nightshades

From bittersweet to henbane, the nightshades advertise their presence with bright flowers and large shiny berries. All of them are poisonous, but some have been adapted for use in medicines.

It may come as a surprise to discover that the nightshades belong to the potato family – the Solanaceae. The best-known member of the group, deadly nightshade, produces dark cherry-like fruits, just two or three of which can kill a child if eaten. All plants in this group are poisonous to a degree but the tubers or fruits of some species, such as potato, tomato and chilli pepper, are edible.

Tropical origins
Members of the Solanaceae family are mainly native to the warm temperate and tropical regions of the Southern Hemisphere, especially South America. Most of the British and Irish nightshades have been introduced or spread by human activity.

The plants are extremely varied, but the dozen or so species that grow in Britain and Ireland are recognisable as a group. Some are shrubby or perennial, while those associated with cultivated land or wasteground are mostly annual or biennial.

The leaves are usually large, often oval, unlobed or deeply lobed and jaggedly toothed. The conspicuous flowers are solitary or borne in small, branched clusters. Each has five fused sepals with five lobes or teeth. The flowers, each with five fused petals, are bell, funnel or disc-shaped.

The disc-shaped flowers have distinct, spreading petal lobes, which tend to bend back as the flower matures. Five male stamens surround the female pollen-catching stigma. In bittersweet and the annual nightshades, the stamens form a prominent yellow cone in the flower centre. The many-seeded fruit is a fleshy berry or, in henbane, a dry capsule that splits when ripe. In some species, the fruit is partly or wholly enclosed by the enlarged fused sepals.

Deadly cocktail
Nightshades are poisonous and, apart from the well-known vegetables, all members of this family are best left alone. It is worth remembering that even potato tubers can become poisonous if they are exposed to light and turn green. Deadly nightshade contains three alkaloids – atropine, hyoscyamine and scopolamine. These nitrogen-containing chemicals affect the nervous system. Atropine is still used by ophthalmologists to dilate the pupil of the eye and is also a constituent of some medicines used to treat diarrhoea. Henbane has long been used as a sedative and anaesthetic.

◄ **Henbane, which occasionally appears on chalk grassland, contains hyoscyamine and scopolamine. It was used by the infamous Dr Crippen to murder his wife in 1910.**

▲ **The berries of the deadly nightshade are highly toxic. The plant flourishes on disturbed soils such as rabbit warrens, old quarries and forest tracks.**

NIGHTSHADES FACT FILE

● **Deadly nightshade**
Atropa belladonna
Habitat and distribution
Woodland clearings, scrub and wasteground on lime-rich soils, mainly in south
Size Up to 2m (6½ft) tall
Key features
A stout, erect, often downy perennial; leaves pointed oval, untoothed, stalked; flowers dull purple, solitary, bell-shaped, 25–30mm (1–1¼in) long; fruit a large black, glossy berry
Flowering time
June–August

● **Black nightshade**
Solanum nigrum
Habitat and distribution
Weed of cultivated land mainly in south and east England; rare in Scotland and Ireland
Size Up to 70cm (2ft 4in) tall
Key features
A bushy, variably downy annual; stems often blackish purple; leaves pointed oval or diamond-shaped, untoothed or coarsely toothed, stalked; flowers white, disc-shaped, 10–14mm (⅜–⅝in) across, in clusters of 5–10; fruits small, usually black, glossy berries
Flowering time
July–September

● **Leafy-fruited nightshade**
Solanum sarachoides
Habitat and distribution
Weed of rubbish tips, cultivated land and wasteground on light soils in south
Size Up to 40cm (16in) tall
Key features
Similar to black nightshade, but fruits green and enclosed by enlarged calyx
Flowering time
July–September

● **Hairy nightshade**
Solanum villosum
Habitat and distribution
Scarce on cultivated and waste-ground in southern England
Size Up to 60cm (2ft) tall
Key features
Similar to black nightshade, but leaves more deeply lobed, softly hairy; fruits red, orange or yellow
Flowering time
July–September

● **Bittersweet or woody nightshade**
Solanum dulcamara
Habitat and distribution
Woodland margins, scrub, fens, ditches and coastal shingle
Size Stems up to 3m (10ft) long
Key features
Hairless scrambling perennial, woody stems; leaves dark green, pointed oval, lowest usually divided into 3; flowers violet-purple, disc-shaped, in clusters; fruit a scarlet berry
Flowering time
June–September

● **Small nightshade**
Solanum triflorum
Habitat and distribution
A scarce weed of cultivated land in eastern England
Size Stems up to 40cm (16in) long
Key features
Similar to black nightshade, but leaves deeply cut; flowers in clusters of 2–3; fruits green marbled with white
Flowering time
August–September

Deadly nightshade
Atropa belladonna

Black nightshade
Solanum nigrum

Leafy-fruited nightshade
Solanum sarachoides

Small nightshade
Solanum triflorum

Bittersweet or woody nightshade
Solanum dulcamara

Hairy nightshade
Solanum villosum

NIGHTSHADES FACT FILE

● Henbane
Hyoscyamus niger
Habitat and distribution
Bare, sandy, disturbed and manured ground, especially near the sea; sometimes on chalky grassland
Size Up to 1m (3ft) tall
Key features
An erect, leafy, sticky-downy, foul-smelling biennial; leaves oval, lobed or deeply toothed, stalked; flowers dull creamy yellow with purplish veins, funnel-shaped, in 2 rows, 20–30mm (¾–1¼in) across; fruit a conical capsule
Flowering time
June–August

● Duke of Argyll's teaplant
Lycium barbarum
Habitat and distribution
Planted as a hedge, especially on south coasts; rare and coastal in the north
Size Stems up to 2.8m (9ft 2in) long
Key features
A hairless, straggling shrub with arched, often spiny stems; leaves slightly greyish green, strap-shaped, untoothed; flowers pale purplish, 10–15mm (⅜–⅝in) across, solitary or 2–3 together; fruit an oval red berry
Flowering time
June–September

● Cock's-eggs
Salpichroa origanifolia
Habitat and distribution
Naturalised in a few bushy and waste places along south and east coasts
Size Stems up to 2m (6½ft) long
Key features
A branched, scrambling perennial, woody at base; leaves oval, blunt, untoothed, stalked; flowers white, bell-shaped, solitary, 6–10mm (¼–½in) long; fruit an egg-shaped, creamy white pineapple-scented berry
Flowering time
August–September

● Thorn-apple
Datura stramonium
Habitat and distribution
Occasionally abundant on disturbed or cultivated land, mostly in southeastern England
Size Up to 1m (3ft) tall
Key features
A robust, erect, leafy, foul-smelling annual; leaves oval, ragged-toothed, up to 30cm (1ft) long; flowers white or pale purple, trumpet-shaped, 50–100mm (2–4in) long, solitary; fruit an erect, spiny, conker-like capsule
Flowering time
July–October

Originally grown as hedging, Duke of Argyll's teaplant has become naturalised in nearby hedges and scrub. The small, purple flowers are followed by scarlet, egg-shaped berries, which are popular with birds but mildly poisonous to humans.

Henbane
Hyoscyamus niger

Duke of Argyll's teaplant
Lycium barbarum

Cock's eggs
Salpichroa origanifolia

WILDLIFE WATCH

Where do nightshades grow?

● Most nightshades occur on cultivated ground, wasteground and waysides, or among old ruins. Some, such as thorn-apple, appear sporadically in hot summers. Others, such as henbane, may suddenly appear on disturbed soil.

● Woody nightshade is a plant of hedgerows and damp places and may be found in neglected gardens. Deadly nightshade is more specialised and grows in some woodland clearings and hedges on chalk and limestone.

Thorn-apple
Datura stramonium

DANGER!

All these plants are poisonous, especially deadly nightshade and henbane. Wash your hands if you have touched any part of the plant – but the best advice is to leave them alone.

Recognising grassland fungi

A hillside dotted with scarlet, yellow and orange waxcaps is a delightful sight on a damp morning, while in paddocks and pastures the satin caps of field and horse mushrooms glisten in the wet grass.

Hundreds of different fungi, including some colourful, large and bizarre-looking species, grow on lawns and hillsides, in the damp hollows of dunes and in churchyards and city parks all over the country.

Such grassland is a difficult environment for organisms as fragile as fungi because, unlike flowers and grasses, they have little to protect them from the wind and direct sunshine. In order to prevent drying out, some species, the waxcaps for instance, have evolved a thick waxy skin, while the fairy-ring champignon has developed a tough texture similar to cartilage. One species, the barometer earth-star, even has 'petals' that curl up in dry weather and spread wide when it rains.

Unlike woodland fungi, which often live in partnership with trees, most grassland species are free-living, feeding on rotting matter in the soil. They tend to be small, with some spectacular exceptions. The parasol mushroom and the horse mushroom can grow to the size of a hat, and giant puffballs the size of footballs are not unusual – a particularly big puffball was once mistaken for a dead sheep. Very large fungi prefer rich, well-manured soil. They are often found in association with clumps of nettles.

Fruits and spores

The 'fruit' of the fungi – the part seen above ground – appears once a year, usually in the autumn. Spores are scattered from the gills, which

◄ Shaggy parasols often grow in clusters. They tolerate areas, such as parks and commons, that are sometimes trampled.

▲ The fairy-ring champignon is common on lawns and in parks, especially in autumn. This mushroom is edible, but similar-looking species that do not form rings are poisonous.

are located under the cap. The giant puffball cracks open to release billions of spores, which are dispersed by the wind. This strategy would not work so well in the enclosed spaces of woodland, but out in open fields the fungus can let the breeze do all the work.

Splashes of colour

Land that has not been treated with nitrate fertilisers, which kill many fungi, sometimes supports scarce, colourful examples, such as the pinkgills. One of this group has a midnight-blue cap. The rarer earth tongues, which may occasionally be found protruding from the turf, are black or green.

Almost all the common and edible species of mushroom and toadstool that grow in grassland have similar counterparts that are at best inedible, and at worst very poisonous. Remember that fungi are notoriously variable in their appearance and always be absolutely sure of the identification before you eat any collected in the wild – if in any doubt, leave them alone. Also avoid eating any collected near a road because they may have picked up toxins from the fumes of passing traffic.

EASY GUIDE TO SPOTTING GRASSLAND FUNGI

WHAT ARE GRASSLAND FUNGI?

● For much of the year, fungi live as a rambling mass, called the mycelium, which is made up of microscopic threads (hyphae) that are interwoven into thicker, whitish threads known as rhizomorphs. The mycelium is usually hidden from view beneath the ground or in decaying wood. It is the vegetative part of the fungus that feeds by breaking down organic matter, from animal droppings to dead leaves, or by taking nutrients from plant roots. Arising from the mycelium, the mushrooms or toadstools that are seen above ground are the fruiting bodies, in which sexual reproduction takes place and seed-like spores are produced to continue the cycle. Spores are transported by insects or the wind and most of them die, but some survive to form a new mycelium elsewhere.

● Most grassland fungi belong to the major class Basidiomycota and are known as basidiomycetes. Their spores are produced, usually in groups of four, on the outside of microscopic club-like structures, the basidia. Most grassland basidiomycetes have the familiar mushroom shape, with a distinct cap at the top of a stem. Many belong to the agarics, which bear their spores, protected by gills, beneath the cap.

● Although most grassland fungi belong to the class Basidiomycota, some are members of the class Ascomycota, with spores that develop within microscopic flask-shaped structures (called asci) in the fruiting body, usually in groups of eight. Grassland ascomycetes include the grey or brown brain-like morels, usually found near shrubs or trees, and the earth-tongues, with tongue-shaped black or olive-green fruit bodies.

● There is no biological difference between mushrooms and toadstools. Edible fungi are generally referred to as mushrooms.

HOW CAN I IDENTIFY GRASSLAND FUNGI?

● The parasol mushrooms, inkcaps, waxcaps and puffballs are all very distinctive in appearance. Waxcaps are almost flower-like in their bright colours as they dot a sheep-grazed grassy hillside. Closer to, they resemble little pieces of bright red, orange, yellow, pink, violet or green shiny plastic, with waxy coatings that prevent their surface from drying out in strong upland breezes. To distinguish species, look for features such as the shape of the cap, the colour or pattern of colours on it, whether or not the cap blackens, and the colour of the gills, remembering that, as with other fungi, these features change with age.

● Grassland fungi may not grow on the same sites each year, often appearing in different places depending on weather and spore dispersal.

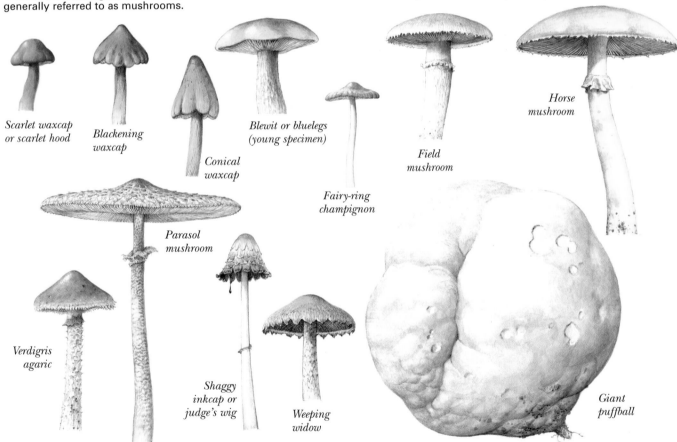

Scarlet waxcap or scarlet hood

Blackening waxcap

Conical waxcap

Blewit or bluelegs (young specimen)

Fairy-ring champignon

Field mushroom

Horse mushroom

Parasol mushroom

Verdigris agaric

Shaggy inkcap or judge's wig

Weeping widow

Giant puffball

WILDLIFE WATCH

Where can I see grassland fungi?

● Any fields grazed by sheep, cattle or horses will usually have fungi. Dung roundheads, for instance, grow on cow pats. Limestone hill pastures are especially good places to look for them.

● Country churchyards, lawns and grounds of stately homes and other old houses are often scattered with fungi.

● Waxcaps grow on unimproved grassland, especially hillsides and heaths, among sand dunes and along clifftops in many parts of the country. They also flourish in some gardens, parks and churchyards. The best sites for them are well-drained areas that are regularly grazed or mowed to maintain short turf, low levels of nitrogen and a flourishing layer of mosses.

● Urban grassy areas, such as parks and verges, may support parasols, inkcaps and some other fungi.

● Although the best season for grassland fungi is autumn, a spell of warm, wet weather lasting longer than a week at any time of year is likely to encourage the fungus fruiting bodies to start pushing up above ground.

SCARLET WAXCAP OR SCARLET HOOD *Hygrocybe coccinea*

One of the most brilliantly coloured of all grassland fungi, the scarlet waxcap is found all over the country. The bell-shaped cap often has yellowish edges, and does not change colour or blacken unless damaged. The tiny lumps on the cap and lack of streaks on the stem are distinctive.

The upper surface of the cap is greasy to the touch. When wet with rain, it feels slimy.

● **SIZE**
Cap 2–4cm (¾–1½in) across; stem 2–5cm (¾–2in)

● **KEY FEATURES**
Bright tomato red cap; gills pale yellow at first, turning blood-red with age; stem same colour as cap or more orange, and paler at base; related species smaller or more orange and paler at base

● **SEASON**
Fruits from late summer through to early winter

● **HABITAT**
Unfertilised grassland in meadows and on verges and lawns; also occasionally on grass banks, especially at edges of woods

● **DISTRIBUTION**
Common on suitable sites

BLACKENING WAXCAP *Hygrocybe nigrescens*

Initially with an orange or red cap, this poisonous waxcap slowly darkens with age until it looks burnt. If damaged or cut, it can turn entirely black within hours. The bell-shaped, irregularly lobed cap spreads out and becomes waxy as the fungus matures.

Conical at first, the cap broadens with age into a more flattened shape but it retains its central point as a hump, or umbo.

● **SIZE**
Cap 3.5–5.5cm (1⅜–2¼in) across; stem 3–7cm (1¼–2¾in)

● **KEY FEATURES**
Orange or red cap that fades and blackens with age and on handling, conical at first but becomes flatter; gills pale yellow, blacken later; stem yellowish, tinged red, paler at base, streaked black later

● **SEASON**
Fruits late summer to late autumn; often appears after rain

● **HABITAT**
Unfertilised grassland, usually short grass in meadows, pastures, churchyards, on lawns and verges; also grass in open woodland

● **DISTRIBUTION**
Widespread but often infrequent

CONICAL WAXCAP *Hygrocybe conica*

In common with several British waxcap species, this one blackens with age or when bruised, but not as markedly or quickly as the blackening waxcap. It can also be distinguished from the often larger blackening waxcap by its more acutely conical shape. The edge of its cap is irregularly lobed.

The steeply conical cap broadens somewhat with age but retains its central point.

● **SIZE**
Cap 2–5cm (¾–2in) across; stem 2–6cm (¾–2½in)

● **KEY FEATURES**
Steeply conical cap, bright orange-red, blackens slowly with age or damage; gills pale yellow, tinged greyish; stem yellowish orange, often darkening at base; inedible, and may be poisonous

● **SEASON**
Fruits from late summer to autumn

● **HABITAT**
Unfertilised grassland, often in short mown or grazed grass, including lawns, parks, churchyards, verges of roads and sometimes on edges of woodland

● **DISTRIBUTION**
Common on suitable sites

BLEWIT OR BLUELEGS *Lepista personata*

This medium-sized agaric mushroom is relatively easy to recognise, with its combination of a beige cap that is flat and wavy-edged when mature and a shortish, thick, lilac-coloured stem with a swollen base. Like its relative the wood blewit, it can be found growing late in the year.

Highly valued for the table, this fungus may be found growing in groups, sometimes in rings.

● **SIZE**
Cap 6–14cm (2½–5½in) across; stem 4–8cm (1½–3in)

● **KEY FEATURES**
Pale brown cap, at first convex and then becoming flattened and finally bowl-shaped with wavy edges; thick buff or whitish flesh, pinkish buff gills; stout bluish lilac stem with no ring; strong, pleasant aroma

● **SEASON**
Fruits in late autumn to winter

● **HABITAT**
Pastures, verges and parkland, often in grass under trees; occasionally in woodland

● **DISTRIBUTION**
Becoming scarce in many areas

FAIRY-RING CHAMPIGNON — *Marasmius oreades*

These small, delightfully named agaric mushrooms grow in the classic fairy-ring formation, as well as in arcs. Rings are small and ill-defined when the fungi are young. Although this mushroom is edible, it looks very similar to other small brown grassland fungi that are poisonous, so positive identification is vital.

The edge of the mushroom's cap is tough and leathery, and fluted like a pie crust.

- **SIZE**
Cap 2–5cm (¾–2in) across; stem 2–10cm (¾–4in)

- **KEY FEATURES**
Cap tan colour when damp, paler with tan tinge at centre when dry, domed at first, flattening with a broad bump in the centre with age; pale gills widely spaced, almost free from stem, which is tough, stiff and dry

- **SEASON**
Fruits late spring to late autumn, often after rain

- **HABITAT**
Short grass in parks, pastures, meadows and on lawns, verges, sports grounds

- **DISTRIBUTION**
Widespread; generally common, especially in autumn

FIELD MUSHROOM — *Agaricus campestris*

These are the best known of all edible wild mushrooms and may still be found in large groups or even rings. Beware of confusing them with the poisonous yellow-stainer, which has a more prominent stem ring and a base that turns yellow when cut or bruised.

The field mushroom's cap is usually silky smooth but may develop fine scales with age. Its flesh sometimes turns pink when cut.

- **SIZE**
Cap 3–10cm (1¼–4in) across; stem 3–10cm (1¼–4in)

- **KEY FEATURES**
Cap creamy white, may have yellowish tinge, turning pinkish grey with age; rounded at first, becoming flatter; stem short, cylindrical or tapering, with fragile ring; gills deep pink at first, turning chocolate brown

- **SEASON**
Fruits from late summer all through autumn, especially in warm, misty weather

- **HABITAT**
Well-manured pasture, open fields and grass verges

- **DISTRIBUTION**
Widespread; still common where traditional mixed farming provides manure

HORSE MUSHROOM — *Agaricus arvensis*

Highly regarded for its flavour, this mushroom differs from the field mushroom in retaining a large, fleshy, pendant ring with a cogwheel-like pattern beneath. The thick white flesh slowly bruises yellow, but unlike the poisonous yellow stainer, it has an aniseed smell, not a carbolic or inky one.

A mature horse mushroom may have a cap as large as a dinner plate.

- **SIZE**
Cap 8–20cm (3–8in) or more across; stem 8–15cm (3–6in)

- **KEY FEATURES**
Large, robust mushroom with white or cream cap, yellowing slightly with age or bruising; stem slightly club-shaped, ring with patterned lower layer of tissue; gills white at first, then pink, then dark brown or blackish

- **SEASON**
Fruits from late summer all through autumn and into winter, peaking in September

- **HABITAT**
Pasture, especially grazed by horses, meadows, parks, gardens and near broad-leaved woods

- **DISTRIBUTION**
Frequent in suitable sites

VERDIGRIS AGARIC — *Stropharia aeruginosa*

The sight of a group of these medium-sized agarics always attracts attention due to their unusual colour. This colour is confined to the skin and is water-soluble, so may be washed out by rain. The aniseed funnel mushroom is a similar colour but lacks a stem ring.

The striking blue-green colour of this poisonous fungus and its close relatives is distinctive but becomes paler with age.

- **SIZE**
Cap 2–8cm (¾–3in) across; stem 4–10cm (1½–4in)

- **KEY FEATURES**
Cap slimy, blue-green, with fleecy white scales at the edge when young; gills white, then brown with white-frosted edge, unlike the similar blue roundhead; stem has white woolly scales below ring

- **SEASON**
Fruits from late summer to autumn

- **HABITAT**
Among grass or moss in pastures and other fields, on heathland, or in open woods and woodland edges, on grass and also soil or leaf litter

- **DISTRIBUTION**
Widespread; abundant in suitable sites

PARASOL MUSHROOM *Macrolepiota procera*

In its early stages, the parasol mushroom is club-shaped but the cap soon expands into its mature, wide umbrella form. It resembles the poisonous blusher toadstool, but can be distinguished by its banded stem and double ring that, on older parasols, can be moved up and down the stem.

Tall and elegant, the parasol mushroom is flecked with shaggy brown scales that coalesce to form a dark brown area at the cap's centre.

● SIZE
Cap 10–30cm (4–12in) or more across; stem 15–40cm (6–16in)

● KEY FEATURES
Cap wide, very scaly, pale creamy buff with dull brown scales radiating from centre, where they form a large dark boss, or umbo; gills white; stem very tall, covered with brown scales in bands below double ring

● SEASON
Fruits from late summer all through autumn

● HABITAT
Pasture, meadows, parks, as well as verges, sand-dune grassland, and in clearings and margins of woodland

● DISTRIBUTION
Widespread and generally common

SHAGGY INKCAP OR JUDGE'S WIG *Coprinus comatus*

This is one of the most common species of the inkcap family. Its alternative name refers to the appearance of the tall, mature cap, with its shaggy, curved white scales. As in other inkcaps, its cap and gills dissolve into an inky black liquid after the spores are released.

Shaggy inkcaps grow very quickly and often in large numbers, especially after rain.

● SIZE
Cap 5–15cm (2–6in) tall; stem 10–30cm (4–12in)

● KEY FEATURES
Cap white, adorned with feathery curved scales, club-shaped; gills white at first, turning pink, brown and then black; after release of spores, gills and cap dissolve, leaving just the tall white stem intact

● SEASON
Fruits from late summer to autumn

● HABITAT
Among grass or moss in pastures and fields, on heathland, or in open woods and woodland edges, on grass and also in soil or leaf litter

● DISTRIBUTION
Widespread, often abundant

WEEPING WIDOW *Lacrymaria lacrymabunda*

A member of the same family as the inkcaps, this intriguingly named agaric is so called because its black gills ooze clear droplets like tears in damp weather. Also, when the spores fall, the remnants of the veil (which covered it when it emerged) at the top of the stem become blackened.

Weeping widows often grow in groups among patches of nettles on waste ground.

● SIZE
Cap 4–10cm (1½–4in) across; stem 4–12cm (1½–4¾in)

● KEY FEATURES
Cap yellowish brown, becoming darker, skin has a ragged edge; gills dark brown at first, turning black with pale edges; droplets of water form on gills; stem whitish above with brown tinge below cobweb-like ring remnants

● SEASON
Fruits from early summer to the end of autumn

● HABITAT
Fields and other grassy places, often near buildings or roads; also among grass and leaf litter in woodland

● DISTRIBUTION
Widespread, often abundant

GIANT PUFFBALL *Calvatia gigantea*

The giant puffball is well named because it forms a huge fruiting body – some recorded in Britain have weighed over 20kg (44lb). These great white balls are important for insects, especially flies and beetles, providing them with both food and shelter.

The giant puffball's fruiting body has no stem and is attached to the mycelium by a cord.

● SIZE
10–80cm (4–32in) across

● KEY FEATURES
White, ball-shaped fruiting body slowly turns brown as the spores it contains mature; restraining cord breaks, allowing fruiting body to roll in the wind and rupture, releasing clouds of brown, powdery spores

● SEASON
Fruits from late summer to autumn

● HABITAT
Among grass or moss in pastures and fields, on heathland, or in open woods and woodland edges, on grass and also in soil or leaf litter

● DISTRIBUTION
Uncommon but occasionally frequent

Woodland watch

- Saving the common dormouse
- Recognising bats
- The goldcrest

- The pheasant
- Woodlice
- Plant galls
- Recognising woodland fungi
- Three-pinnate ferns
- Spurges and mercuries

Saving the common dormouse

Felling of hazel woodland has contributed to the drastic decline of this tree-loving creature. Judiciously placed artificial nestboxes are part of a conservation effort to reverse this loss and help the dormouse to survive.

About a hundred years ago, dormice were often found when hedges were trimmed and ditches cleaned out in winter, and children would keep them as pets. Dormice were numerous all over England and Wales, particularly in Midland counties and as far north as Northumberland, a situation reflected in the name 'common' dormouse.

Today, the species is far from common. A 2004 survey estimated that only 40,000 individuals remain in the whole of Britain. The dormouse is absent from much of the Midlands and in Wales it is found in just a few scattered localities. In Suffolk, Bedfordshire, Warwickshire and Northamptonshire, these small mammals inhabit fewer than ten woodlands.

Vanishing habitat

There are several reasons for the dormouse's decline but perhaps the most important is loss of habitat. Dormice need varied woodland with plenty of different shrubs and trees to provide all the fruits, flowers and insects upon which they feed. Like so many other woodland animals, they have suffered as a result of woods being cleared to make way for roads, farms and houses. Roads are a particular problem because they divide large woodlands up into smaller patches. Since dormice do not like to cross roads or other open spaces, they become isolated in the woods that remain. A copse of one hectare (2½ acres) may support just ten adult dormice, which is too few to guarantee long-term survival.

In small isolated copses, dormice also face problems associated with inbreeding. If this native species is to recover, small copses must be linked with hedgerows so that the dormice can travel between them. Existing hedges that form travelling routes must be protected and new hedgerows should be planted. Much of this is now happening, but the destructive activities have been going on for so long, there is much to put right.

Large, forward-facing eyes give the dormouse binocular vision, which enables it to judge distances as it leaps through bushes and trees.

▲ From October to April, the dormouse hibernates alone in a nest it has built among tree roots, at the bottom of a hedge, or in a nestbox. One common cause of death is starvation during hibernation.

Bad weather

As well as losing their habitat, dormice are threatened by the effects of the often dismal British weather. They tend to stay in their nests for longer if it is cold or wet and thus spend less time feeding. In the cool of early summer, they may enter a state of torpor to save energy, as they do when hibernating. In this state, all bodily functions including heart rate are slowed down to just above survival level. This enables the dormouse to withstand low temperatures but it reduces the time available for breeding, which means that dormice cannot raise more than one or two families per year.

▼ The dormouse's bushy tail is one of the main features by which it can be distinguished from other mice. The tail acts as a useful counterbalance when the dormouse is moving through the trees.

HABITAT RESTORATION

Dormice favour woodland with a dense shrub layer and plenty of sunshine, where shrubs can thrive and produce an abundance of food. Shady woodland is not suitable. This may be why dormice have vanished from so many woods in Yorkshire, where mature sycamores cast a shadow over the hazels and hawthorns, the nuts and fruits of which are an important part of the dormouse's diet. Shaded shrubs do not flower or fruit properly so the dormice go hungry and eventually die out.

In many localities across Britain, efforts are being made to thin out overshadowing trees to let in more sunshine. Old hazels are being coppiced, that is pruned and trimmed, in order to rejuvenate them.

The technique goes back hundreds of years and was originally developed in order to produce crops of tall hazel poles. The restoration of this kind of woodland management will benefit the dormouse, provided the hazel is not cut so often it does not have time to produce nuts. Dormice need hazelnuts to fatten up before hibernation. Hazel trees must be at least seven years old to produce a plentiful crop of sizeable nuts, and the best hazel coppice is 10 to 20 years old.

Common hazel
Corylus avellana

The common dormouse is also known as the hazel dormouse because of its preference for hazel coppices. The dense stems protect the rodent's woven nests from the elements and the nuts are a fat-rich source of food.

In autumn, dormice must fatten up on seasonal hedgerow crops if they are to survive the winter. Young born late in the season may not find sufficient food to be able to survive the months of hibernation.

Reintroducing the dormouse

When a species dies out in an area, one possible course of action is to attempt to reintroduce it by releasing a few individuals captured elsewhere. However, this does not work well for the dormouse because the species is already so scarce. If the relocated animals die, nothing is achieved and the dormouse has become rarer still. Moreover, death is very likely if dormice are simply taken to an unfamiliar woodland and released. Their feeding requirements are so specialised that they are likely to starve before they learn where to find food in their new home. Released animals often disperse very quickly, too, which reduces their chances of finding a mate.

To overcome these problems, conservationists use captive breeding programmes to supply dormice for re-introductions, and a special system has been developed for releasing them in a controlled way. Thirty animals or more may be released to ensure that, despite early deaths from tawny owl predation and wet weather, some will survive. The dormice are taken to their new woodland home in the nestboxes in which they were raised. These are installed in special pre-release cages. The dormice remain there for a week or so while they adjust to the sights and sounds of their new location. The cages are then opened, so the animals can move in and out freely.

Settling in

At first, the dormice may explore just the tree in which the cage is sited, but they soon wander farther afield and, with so many animals being released at the same time, their chances of finding a mate are high. Their babies, often born in the nestboxes, are blind and naked at first. They soon grow grey baby fur, but this moults before they leave the nest at around a month old, by which time they resemble adults.

Dormice have an amazing ability to find their way about. After just a week or so, they will take short cuts through the trees in the dark, crossing areas that they have never visited before to get back to their own nestboxes.

The released dormice can return to their cages at any time to feed on fresh fruit and biscuits and to drink water provided for them every day. The extra food means that they have a resource to fall back on while they discover where to find natural food in their new home. Food placed in the boxes also reduces the problem of the dormice dispersing.

PURPOSE-BUILT HOMES

Dormice nestboxes are similar to those provided for blue tits, except that the entrance is placed facing the trunk and should have a bar above and below it to keep the box clear of the tree bark, allowing space for access. Dormice actually seem to prefer to weave their nests in these boxes rather than in bushes and trees. When the weather is wet, cold or windy, a wooden box is clearly better at keeping out the elements than a nest built in branches, and when lined with nesting material makes a very cosy home. Nestboxes are popular for breeding, too, and many baby dormice are born and raised each year in the thousands of nestboxes that have been erected by nature-lovers throughout the woodlands of England and Wales.

Nestboxes are best placed 1.5–2m (5–6½ft) off the ground, attached by wire to the poles of a mature fruiting hazel. Boxes higher up are less likely to be used and those on the ground are avoided – dormice are arboreal and rarely venture below about 1m (3ft), unless building their own nests for winter hibernation.

Inside the box, dormice make their nests from shredded honeysuckle bark. Nestboxes are more likely to be occupied if they are sited close to a honeysuckle plant – a vital nest-building material.

▲ Custom-made dormouse boxes should be placed with the entrance hole facing the tree. The tiny dormice can climb in easily, but most predators are kept out.

▶ The entrance should be small to keep out the wind, rain and predators. The dormouse will nibble it to the perfect size.

▲ A dormouse fills its chosen nestbox with nesting material – mostly stripped honeysuckle bark. It weaves this into a loose ball in much the same way as it would in a natural nest site.

Dormice produce one or occasionally two litters of two to seven young each year. The babies are independent after about a month, when they leave the nest to find homes of their own.

If the animals stay in close proximity they are more likely to breed early, allowing time for their babies to mature and put on weight before winter overtakes them all. The dormice are best released in early summer to allow plenty of time for breeding to occur before they need to hibernate. Once the hazelnuts ripen in August, the artificial feeding can be stopped and the cages taken away, leaving the dormice to fatten up on hazelnuts, blackberries and other autumn crops.

Success stories

Using this method, dormice were released into Cambridgeshire in 1994, where they are now thriving for the first time in nearly a century. In the summer of 1999 a captive-release programme was started to reintroduce dormice to Yorkshire. Some 29 dormice were released in woodlands near Helmsley and 150 nestboxes installed for them. By October,

40 per cent of the boxes had dormice inside. Another success story involves dormice that were rescued from woods being felled to make way for the Channel Tunnel rail link in Kent in 1998. They were released in Warwickshire, which

◄ Dormice construct their compact, woven summer nests in bushes and hedgerows, typically 1.5–2m (5–6½ft) off the ground. Several nests may be found nearby as they often nest in small groups.

▼ Dormice thrive in woodland with a good variety of shrubs and trees to supply a succession of nuts and other fruits and seeds throughout the months of the year when they are active.

until then had only one remaining natural colony of dormice. Now there is another established nearby. More of the rescued Kentish dormice were released, also under controlled conditions, in woodland in north Buckinghamshire.

The stories do not end there, however. Released dormice face great dangers, not least from unseasonably cold or wet weather, which probably kills many of them, especially the young. In addition, the released animals are usually from captive-bred stock and are therefore unfamiliar with the perils posed by predators such as tawny owls. These account for some of the released animals, but those that become wary enough to keep out of trouble and avoid predation can live for up to five years.

Through projects such as these, the dormouse is being put back on the map, but it is too soon to say whether or not these efforts will be successful in the long term. At the very least, some places where the dormouse had become extinct now have these charming little creatures as residents once more.

WILDLIFE WATCH

How can I help dormice?

● Look out for nibbled hazelnuts, in woodland in southern England and report any findings to the Mammal Society and your local Wildlife Trust. You could also join a working party, coppicing areas of hazel woodland to help with the regeneration of the dormouse's favourite habitat.

● Make your own dormouse nestbox and donate it to a local reserve.

● Contact the Mammal Society at 2B Inworth Street, London SW11 3EP (telephone 020 7350 2200 or visit www.mammal.org.uk) for further information about dormice and how you can help.

Recognising bats

Furry bodies and leathery wings give bats their unmistakable appearance, but species can be difficult to tell apart. Clues to the different types of bat lie in the shape of their muzzles and the size of their ears.

Some of the 17 species of bats currently resident in Britain are quite scarce. In fact, several of Britain's rarest mammals are bats – Bechstein's bat, for example. One, the mouse-eared bat, was even thought to have become extinct in 1991, when a lone male failed to return to its hibernation site in Sussex. Since then, however, a few individuals have been recorded, so there is hope for its continued survival.

Bats have a specialised skeleton that supports wing membranes on extended fingers. Another membrane stretches between the hind legs and the tail. The highly modified forelimbs are used as wings. The hind limbs are tiny and used only for hanging upside down in roosts or breeding colonies.

Bats mate in autumn but the embryo does not start to develop until the following spring and the babies are born in June or July. The females choose warm places to have their young – some even use attics and lofts. Cold or wet weather may delay breeding or result in severe losses of young, which is a serious problem because bats reproduce slowly, having a single baby a year. They make up for this by living for a long time, often more than 15 years.

Bats avoid the harshest weather by hibernating in the winter, typically in small groups. They choose from several hibernation sites depending on how cold the weather is. The roosts are usually cool, humid places, such as caves, mines and cellars, although sometimes they choose buildings or trees.

Echoes in the dark

Although bats may sometimes be seen flying in daylight, they are normally nocturnal creatures. They feed on insects that they catch on the wing and they achieve this in the dark by using echo-location. The bats emit bursts of very high-pitched ultrasound – inaudible to the human ear – then listen for the echoes to bounce off solid objects. This form of natural radar produces a detailed sound picture of the bat's surroundings and they also detect minute echoes from flying insects. They seize prey with their teeth or scoop it into the tail membrane. When necessary they do use vision, but their eyesight is relatively poor.

Bats in Britain are all insectivorous. Despite numerous stories, they are completely harmless. They do not damage buildings, get caught in people's hair or spread diseases, and there are no blood-feeding vampire bats in Britain.

Most bats cannot bite humans very effectively, but it is best not to handle them because some can nip and draw blood. All bats are legally protected and may not be captured or disturbed anywhere except in the parts of a house inhabited by humans.

▼ The pipistrelle bat may look fierce, but it is actually very tiny. Note the long forearm and the fleshy prong called the tragus inside the ear. The size and shape of both are important recognition features.

EASY GUIDE TO SPOTTING BATS

Greater horseshoe bat

Horseshoe-shaped fold of skin around the nostrils, projecting up between the eyes

Lesser horseshoe bat

Very small horseshoe structure on face

Noctule

Glossy chestnut fur, blunt face, semi-circular tragus; a big bat

Leisler's bat

Smaller version of noctule with two-tone fur

Barbastelle

Squashed face, thick triangular ears, blackish brown fur

Brown long-eared bat

Huge ears and a blunt muzzle

Serotine

Dark face, bulbous snout, tragus a third of the length of the ear; a big bat

Common pipistrelle

Dark face, blunt tragus; Britain's smallest bat – could fit into a matchbox

Whiskered bat

Dark face, pointed tragus

Daubenton's bat

Pinky brown face, pointed tragus less than half the length of the ear, short muzzle

Natterer's bat

Almost bare, pinkish red skin on face; slender, pointed tragus

Bechstein's bat

Big ears, pointed nose, long tragus; very rare

WHAT ARE BATS?

● Bats belong to the order Chiroptera. They are flying, nocturnal mammals that find their way around using echo-location, occasionally assisted by sight.

● There are 18 families of bats, of which two are represented in the British Isles with two species of horseshoe bats (family Rhinolophidae) and 15 species of vesper bats (family Vespertilionidae).

● All British and Irish species feed on insects but the diet of others worldwide ranges from fruit, nectar and pollen to fish, frogs, and even small reptiles and mammals.

Under the Wildlife and Countryside Act, 1981, bats are legally protected and must not be caught deliberately or disturbed at their roosts or breeding sites.

HOW CAN I IDENTIFY BATS?

● Look carefully at the bat's face. Horseshoe bats have a horseshoe-shaped fold of skin around the nostrils. Vesper bats have a simple, dog-like muzzle and a fleshy growth inside each ear, called the tragus.

● The two groups also differ when resting. Horseshoe bats wrap their wings around the body like a shawl, hanging free by their hind feet. Vesper bats fold their wings alongside the body and hang from their hind feet against a vertical surface, such as a wall or tree.

● The two species of horseshoe bat can be told apart by size. Lesser horseshoes are small enough to hang inside the palm of the hand. Greater horseshoe bats are much larger.

● Vesper bats can be distinguished by the length and shape of the tragus and by accurately measuring the length of the forearm which supports the wing. Sometimes the shape and structure of the tail membrane is another distinguishing characteristic.

● Bats cannot usually be identified reliably when they are in flight. However, noctule (and Leisler's) bats have very narrow wings, at least 30cm (12in) from tip to tip, and they fly fast and high in the early evening. Horseshoe bats have very broad wings and fly slow and low. Long-eared bats have broad wings and a slow flight. Daubenton's bats skim the surface of still water.

Horseshoe bats have rounded wings and a bizarre structure, called the 'nose-leaf', on the nose.

Greater horseshoe bat

Distribution map key

■ Present all year round

□ Not present

GREATER HORSESHOE BAT
Rhinolophus ferrumequinum

Big with broad, rounded wings and a prominent nose-leaf, the greater horseshoe bat is restricted in its distribution. It frequents limestone areas with plenty of caves in which to hibernate over winter. Their slow breeding rate makes them very vulnerable.

A horseshoe bat hangs freely from its hind feet. It has a reddish tinge to the fur on its back.

● **SIZE**
Length 6–7cm (2½–2¾in); wingspan 30–40cm (12–16in); weight 15–35g (½–1¼oz)

● **ROOST**
Caves and tunnels in winter; caves, roof-spaces and other warm spacious cavities in summer

● **BREEDING**
Single young, born late June to late July

● **FOOD**
Large-bodied insects, mainly beetles and moths

● **HABITAT**
Woodlands, hedgerows permanent pasture; prefers steep-sided valleys, close to caves and tunnels

● **DISTRIBUTION**
Rare and largely confined to the south-west (especially Dorset and Devon), Gloucestershire and parts of south Wales; none in Ireland

LESSER HORSESHOE BAT
Rhinolophus hipposideros

A miniature version of the greater horseshoe bat, this is one of Britain's smallest mammals. Its wingspan is two-thirds that of the greater horseshoe and it weighs much less, too. This delicate bat is greatly reduced in numbers and distribution in Europe.

The long, soft fur is usually greyer than that of the greater horseshoe bat. Neither species has a tragus in the ear.

● **SIZE**
Length 3.5–4cm (1⅜–1½in); wingspan 20–25cm (8–10in); weight 4–9g (about ¼oz)

● **ROOST**
Caves, tunnels and cellars in winter; roof-spaces of large rural houses and outbuildings in summer

● **BREEDING**
Single young, born late June or early July

● **FOOD**
Caddis flies, midges, craneflies and moths

● **HABITAT**
Woodland and forest edges, pastureland

● **DISTRIBUTION**
Now very local in distribution; found in Wales, parts of western Ireland and south-west England; once found as far north as Yorkshire

NOCTULE
Nyctalus noctula

Bats seen flying in the early evening, often before the sun has set, are likely to be noctules. They have long, narrow wings and usually fly at treetop height. The broad muzzle, semi-circular tragus and big, thick ears are features also seen in Leisler's bat.

A big, common bat with short rounded ears and a bare face, the noctule's fur is short and glossy.

● **SIZE**
Length 6.5–8cm (2½–3in); wingspan 33–45cm (13–18in); weight 20–45g (¾–1½oz)

● **ROOST**
Tree holes in winter; breeds in tree holes and bat boxes in summer

● **BREEDING**
Single young, born late June or early July

● **FOOD**
Midges in spring; large-bodied insects, such as moths, in summer

● **HABITAT**
Feeds high over woodland, pasture and water, making dramatic steep dives to snatch prey nearer the ground

● **DISTRIBUTION**
Widespread in England and Wales, north to southern Scotland; stragglers in northern Scotland, none in Ireland

LEISLER'S BAT
Nyctalus leisleri

Leisler's bat is similar to the noctule, but smaller. The forearm is at most 4.7cm (1⅞in) long – in noctules it is up to 5.8cm (2¼in). Leisler's bat occurs in Ireland, but is rare in Britain. Its fur is longer, and spreads more along the underside of the wing, than in the noctule.

The upper fur is dark at the base, paler red-brown at the tips.

● **SIZE**
Length 5–6.8cm (2–2¾in); wingspan 26–32cm (10½–12¾in); weight 11–20g (¼–¾oz)

● **ROOST**
Probably tree holes in winter, but very rarely seen; woodpecker holes, bat boxes and hollow trees in summer; sometimes breeds in roof-spaces

● **BREEDING**
Single young, born late June or early July

● **FOOD**
Craneflies, midges, moths and beetles

● **HABITAT**
Flies straight and fast, often over open pasture and water in early evening

● **DISTRIBUTION**
Common in Ireland, but rare elsewhere; patchy distribution in England and southern Scotland

BARBASTELLE *Barbastella barbastellus*

The blackish fur of the barbastelle bat is tipped with creamy white, giving the coat a distinctive frosted appearance. The ears are short and broad, so that the front edges touch each other at the base above the forehead. The tragus is almost triangular.

The barbastelle's peculiar flattened face looks as though the bat has just flown into a brick wall.

● SIZE
Length 4–5.5cm (1½–2¼in); wingspan 26–29cm (10½–11½in); weight 6–13g (⅛–½oz)

● ROOST
Only comes into sheltered caves, mines and buildings in very cold weather; hibernates mainly in deep hollows in old or storm-damaged trees; in summer it roosts in cracks in trees

● BREEDING
Single young born late June or early July

● FOOD
Small insects, mainly moths, caught in flight

● HABITAT
Wooded areas and river valleys; often feeds over water

● DISTRIBUTION
Widespread but patchy in southern England and Wales; none in Ireland

BROWN LONG-EARED BAT *Plecotus auritus*

The brown (or common) long-eared bat is one of the most common species. It is the only British mammal with ears as long as its head and body. Grey long-eared bats (*Plecotus austriacus*) also occur in Britain, but are very rare. They have greyer fur than the brown long-eared and a broader tragus.

The brown long-eared bat is agile and can fly much more slowly than other bats.

● SIZE
Length 3.7–5.3cm (1½–2¼in); wingspan 24–28cm (9½–11in); weight 5–12g (¼–½oz)

● ROOST
Hibernates in tunnels, cellars, mines and caves in winter; may often be found in large roof-spaces, barns and churches in summer, as well as hollow trees and bat boxes

● BREEDING
Single young, born June

● FOOD
Moths, caterpillars, spiders and other insects gleaned from the surface of leaves; insects also taken in flight

● HABITAT
Feeds around trees, bushes or hedges in farmland, parks, gardens and woodland

● DISTRIBUTION
Common throughout Britain and also in Ireland

SEROTINE *Eptesicus serotinus*

This is a large southern species, only rarely recorded north of the Midlands. It often roosts in wall cavities, but is less abundant now than 20 years ago. It is the only British bat in which the last joint of the tail projects beyond the edge of the tail membrane.

The serotine has long, dark brown fur, often with paler tips to the hairs. Its face and ears are very dark.

● SIZE
Length 6.5–8cm (2½–3in); wingspan 31.5–38cm (12½–15in); weight 15–30g (½–1oz)

● ROOST
All year round in old buildings and under floors; in summer found in roof-spaces, cavity walls and small nooks and crannies

● BREEDING
Nursery colonies begin to form in May; females produce one young each in early July

● FOOD
Large beetles, flies and moths, sometimes snatched from the ground

● HABITAT
Flies around trees and over pastureland

● DISTRIBUTION
Widespread from Devon to Kent, petering out in the Midlands and eastern Wales; none in Ireland

COMMON PIPISTRELLE *Pipistrellus pipistrellus*

The most common British bat is also the smallest. The fur is a uniform colour, but this varies from place to place and may be orange-brown or greyish, and is usually paler below. The tragus is about half the height of the ear. Soprano and Nathusius's pipistrelles also live in Britain.

The pipistrelle has a rapid flight and can change direction abruptly.

● SIZE
Length 3.5–4.5cm (1⅜–1¾in); wingspan 18–25cm (7–10in); weight 4–8g (about ¼oz)

● ROOST
Sometimes seen among stonework in winter; attics and roof-spaces in summer, rarely in trees

● BREEDING
Large nursery colonies form from May; females have single young in June to mid-July

● FOOD
Midges and tiny flies caught on the wing

● HABITAT
All habitats except highest uplands; common even in urban areas

● DISTRIBUTION
Common all over Britain and Ireland; soprano pipistrelle also common; Nathusius's probably rare but widespread

WHISKERED BAT *Myotis mystacinus*

This species has a cousin called Brandt's bat (*Myotis brandtii*), which is so similar to the whiskered bat that it was not identified as a separate species until 1970. Both are widespread and can be identified by the tragus which is thin, long and sharply pointed.

The whiskered bat is small, with a very dark face and pointed ears. Adults have a creamy white or buff belly.

● SIZE
Length 3.5–4.8cm (1⅜–2in); wingspan 21–24cm (8¼–9½in); weight 4–8g (about ¼oz)

● ROOST
Usually hibernates in cool places underground in winter, often solitary; in summer enters buildings, including houses, churches and farm outbuildings

● BREEDING
Single young, born in June or early July

● FOOD
Small insects usually caught in flight, but also spiders picked from foliage

● HABITAT
Woodlands, parks, gardens, farmland and over water

●
DISTRIBUTION
Occurs throughout England, Wales and Ireland (most common in west), and in part of southern Scotland

DAUBENTON'S BAT *Myotis daubentonii*

A medium-sized bat with a pinkish brown face and blunt nose (not pointed as in the whiskered bat, which it resembles). The ears are pink at the base and too short to fold forward to reach the tip of the nose, unlike those of whiskered bats.

The forearm, prominent here, is a useful guide. In Daubenton's bat its average length is slightly more than in the whiskered bat.

● SIZE
Length 4.5–5.5cm (1¾–2¼in); wingspan 24–27.5cm (9½–10¾in); weight 7–14g (¼–½oz)

● ROOST
Hibernates in caves and other underground sites in winter; tree holes, tunnels, and buildings, sometimes in cracked stonework of old bridges in summer

● BREEDING
Single young, born late June

● FOOD
Midges, caddisflies, mayflies and small moths, caught flying low over water

● HABITAT
Close to water, where it skims the surface in search of food

●
DISTRIBUTION
Widespread and fairly common in Britain and Ireland but patchy and less numerous in Scotland

NATTERER'S BAT *Myotis nattereri*

The baggy tail of Natterer's bat is used to help it catch prey in flight. The ears are pink at the base and long enough to fold forwards and wrap around the end of the bat's nose (distinguishing it from Daubenton's and whiskered bats, which might easily be confused with this species).

Natterer's is a medium-sized bat with a pure white underside and brick-red face.

● SIZE
Length 4–5cm (1½–2in); wingspan 25–30cm (10–12in); weight 5–12g (⅛–¼oz)

● ROOST
Hibernates late in crevices in caves, mines and other underground places in winter; found in roof-spaces, walls or among timbers of old buildings in summer

● BREEDING
Single young, born late June or early July

● FOOD
Mainly moths and flies, also beetles, spiders and caterpillars, often picked off leaves of trees

● HABITAT
Parkland, open woodlands and farmland; sometimes feeds low over water

● DISTRIBUTION
Common and widespread in southern Britain, increasingly scarce further north

BECHSTEIN'S BAT *Myotis bechsteini*

Few breeding sites are known for this rare species. It is best identified by its ears, which are so large that it cannot be confused except with long-eared bats. However, Bechstein's ears have a smooth edge while those of long-eared bats have a prominent swelling on the front edges.

Bechstein's bat has a pointed tragus and muzzle as well as long ears.

● SIZE
Length 4.3–5cm (1¾–2in); wingspan 25–30cm (10–12in); weight 7–14g (¼–½oz)

● ROOST
Occasionally found in caves and mines in winter; may also hibernate in tree holes; woodpecker holes and hollow trees in summer

● BREEDING
Single young born in late July and early August

● FOOD
Mainly moths, taken in the air or from leaves of trees

● HABITAT
Mainly in woodland and close to water

● DISTRIBUTION
Rare but increasingly recorded at scattered sites in the south of England and Wales

The goldcrest

These exotic-looking birds raise a brightly coloured crest when alarmed and utter high-pitched warning calls. Constantly on the move, they are expert at concealing themselves from predators high up in the branches of coniferous trees.

Goldcrests are among the most subtly beautiful of British birds. They have olive green plumage and a startling crown stripe, which is lemon yellow in females and touched with flame orange in males.

This tiny creature is the smallest native British (and European) breeding bird – individuals weigh just five or six grams, which equates to about five birds to the ounce. A goldcrest flitting about in a conifer plantation might almost be mistaken for a large moth.

The goldcrest's lightweight stature enables it to dart among the branches, gleaning tiny insects and other invertebrates from the foliage of trees and bushes. It examines crevices in the bark of trees in a similar way to the treecreeper. While searching for food, these agile birds frequently hang upside down or hover to pick insects from the undersides of leaves with their sharp beaks. Prey is usually taken from the outer tips of tree branches but when it snows, goldcrests will visit the ground to peck insects and seeds from the surface of the snow.

Long migration

It is amazing to think of such tiny birds making long migratory flights across the open sea but many goldcrests do just that. The resident population amounts to around one million breeding pairs but every autumn this count is swollen by large numbers of immigrants from northern Europe. Goldcrests from as far east as the Baltic, Finland and even Russia migrate across the North Sea to spend the winter in Britain. Research involving ringing birds has shown that the birds can cover 1000km (600 miles) in less than a week.

On reaching British shores, the birds may adopt a fairly nomadic existence or settle down with a resident group of fellow goldcrests. The itinerant visitors are likely to turn up almost anywhere. They quite often visit suburban gardens, and have even been seen coming to feed on balls of fat or suet put out on a bird table.

When foraging for insects, goldcrests move quickly among the pine needles, sometimes hovering to access awkwardly positioned prey. The needle-thin bill acts like a pair of tweezers to seize insects and spiders.

GOLDCREST FACT FILE

More often heard than seen, the tiny goldcrest is found mainly in northern coniferous forests although it has become more widespread due to the planting of conifers in other areas. It is a prolific breeder, capable of producing up to 20 nestlings in just one season.

● NAMES
Common name: goldcrest
Scientific name: *Regulus regulus*

● HABITAT
Woodlands, especially coniferous; travels widely in winter

● DISTRIBUTION
Throughout Britain and Ireland; absent from parts of the Fens, high mountains and some Scottish islands

● STATUS
Patchily common, with up to 6 breeding pairs per hectare (2½ acres); breeding population over one million pairs following several mild winters; may be as many as 5 million birds in winter, including many immigrants from Europe

● SIZE
Length 8.5–9cm (3½in); weight 5–7g (less than ¼oz)

● KEY FEATURES
Upperparts olive green; underparts buff white; two white wing bars and dark flight feathers; dark eyes set in pale face; crown yellow with black edges in female, orange with black edges in male; juveniles lack crest

● HABITS
Tit-like behaviour; moves restlessly among foliage; often hovers

● VOICE
Song and calls soft and very high-pitched; sweet-sounding song often rendered *'zeebler, zeebler, zeebler, zeebler-der'*; contact call a short *'seee'*

● FOOD
Insects and spiders picked from trees; seeds and insects taken off snow in winter

● BREEDING
Starts late April–early May; 2 broods per year

● NEST
Almost spherical cup of mosses, lichens, cobwebs, feathers and hair; narrow entrance near top; suspended in outer twigs of conifers 15m (50ft) or more from the ground

● EGGS
Smooth and pale with faint markings; clutch size 8–12, laid one a day; incubation by female only; hatch sequentially in 15–17 days

● YOUNG
Brooded by female for 7 days or more; fledge after 18–20 days; fed in the nest by both male and female; last young fledge early August

The goldcrest's nest is carefully built from mosses, lichens and animal hair bound together with spider silk. Hidden among dense foliage, it is difficult to spot.

A black-bordered bright yellow or orange crown is often raised into a slight crest.

The upperparts are a dull greenish colour.

The underparts are buff white.

Greenish wings are marked with two white wing bars.

Strong toes enable the goldcrest to hang upside-down from branches.

Distribution map key

■ Present all year round

□ Present during summer months

□ Present during winter months

□ Not present

If the weather is overcast and misty, with light, south-easterly winds and drizzling rain, the goldcrests may be delayed as they seem to lose their sense of direction in such conditions. On one occasion, when goldcrests were held up by poor weather in Scandinavia, bird observatories such as the one on the Isle of May (off the east coast of Scotland) enjoyed the spectacle of an unprecedented influx of 15,000 birds arriving literally overnight.

Rare companions
The yellow-browed warbler (*Phylloscopus inornatus*) and Pallas's warbler (*Phylloscopus proregulus*) may sometimes

▲ A diet of insect larvae and small spiders helps a family of young goldcrests to grow quickly. Feeding the large brood is an exhausting business undertaken by both parents.

arrive in late autumn with the last of the goldcrests. These birds are barely larger than the goldcrest and share its active habits. They are also similar in appearance, which can occasionally cause confusion, especially as they choose the same bushes and thickets in which to rest during their journey. Both species have greenish upperparts and pale underparts, but the yellow-browed warbler can be

▲ The goldcrest's olive green feathers are beautifully displayed in flight, but unless on migration, the birds seldom fly farther than a few dozen metres. They move from branch to branch searching for small insects and spiders.

distinguished by its pale yellowish eyestripe and double pale yellow wing bars, while Pallas's warbler is strikingly marked with a more prominent yellow crown stripe and a primrose rump patch.

Both birds are rare passage migrants that stop off in Britain, mainly on the east coast, on their way south from their breeding grounds in Siberia. Very specific weather conditions, with high pressure

Non-stop forager

The goldcrest must forage continuously to keep its energy levels up. Flitting from branch to branch, it gleans food from twigs in the crowns of trees. While searching for insects, it will often hang upside down or even hover to peck trapped prey from a spider's web or from the undersides of leaves.

While foraging, the goldcrest often quivers its wings nervously, at the same time posturing and flashing its brightly coloured crown.

The goldcrest's sharp eyes spot a tiny spider hidden against a twig. The tweezer-like bill is ideal for reaching into small crevices.

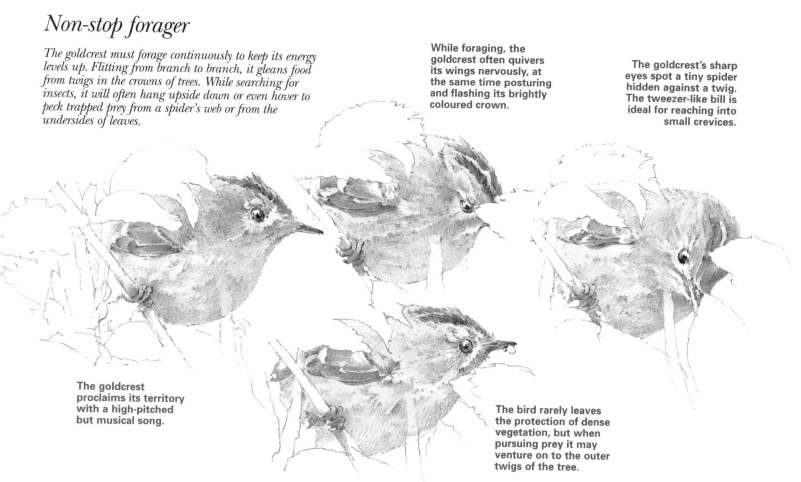

The goldcrest proclaims its territory with a high-pitched but musical song.

The bird rarely leaves the protection of dense vegetation, but when pursuing prey it may venture on to the outer twigs of the tree.

GOLDCREST CALENDAR

JANUARY • FEBRUARY

In the depths of winter, spells of freezing weather that last more than a day or two can be devastating for goldcrests. Roosting birds huddle together for warmth at night.

MARCH • APRIL

By late April, migrant goldcrests will have returned to their breeding grounds in Scandinavia. Resident male birds are busy establishing their territories and singing to attract a mate.

MAY • JUNE

Most first clutches are laid in early May. The chicks are blind at first, their eyes opening after a week. The young from the first brood fledge in June and the second brood is started immediately.

JULY • AUGUST

While the parent birds are busy raising their second brood, young birds from the first clutch move around the woodland, mixing with foraging flocks of tits and warblers.

SEPTEMBER • OCTOBER

Birds from Scandinavia start to arrive in earnest in late September and most migrants have reached the eastern coast of Britain by the end of October. Local birds also begin to move around.

NOVEMBER • DECEMBER

Peak migration draws to an end in early November, but with numbers greatly boosted, the flocks of birds are very nomadic. They may travel long distances to find suitable feeding sites.

building up across Eastern Europe into Asia, are required for them to reach Britain's shores.

Nests and eggs

The breeding season starts in late April or May. The male displays his orange and yellow crest to attract his chosen mate, after which each pair builds a cosy little hammock nest in the outer twigs of a conifer tree or bush.

The male does more construction work than the female and the pair may spend as long as three weeks completing the nest – other pairs may hurriedly put it together in a matter of days. The nest is almost completely spherical and has three distinct layers, which means it is well insulated and warm.

The outer layer is made of cobwebs, lichens and mosses, skilfully anchored to living twigs. More mossy material forms the middle layer while the inner lining consists of soft hair and feathers.

Goldcrests can sometimes be seen bathing in shallow puddles. Feather care is imperative – the birds' small size means that they lose heat easily, so their plumage must be kept in good condition for maximum insulation.

One egg is laid into this snug ball every morning. The female goldcrest can lay up to a dozen eggs. Although tiny, the eggs weigh up to 14 per cent of the adult female's body weight, so the whole clutch may weigh more than one and a half times her full body weight. Studies suggest that bigger eggs are laid at the end of the clutch. It is not fully understood why this

is the case, but it could be that when the female lays her first few eggs, she is still putting the finishing touches to the nest. By the time she lays her last eggs, the nest is complete, so she has more time to devote to feeding herself. The energy obtained from her food can be invested in larger eggs. Egg size also tends to increase during periods of warm weather.

THE FIRECREST

The firecrest, *Regulus ignicapillus*, is a little larger than the goldcrest but this is barely noticeable. The species is more easily distinguished by its greener upperparts, whiter underparts, a piratical eyestripe and the bronze wash over the 'shoulders'. The firecrest's call is slightly more metallic than that of the goldcrest, and its song is louder and does not speed up to a final trill. Firecrests and goldcrests are so closely related that where the two species co-exist they will even interbreed.

Both species inhabit a large area of central Europe. The firecrest prefers open deciduous or mixed woodland while the goldcrest lives in dense coniferous forests. In some areas, the firecrest inhabits gardens, making do with exotic conifers.

In Britain, firecrests are much rarer than goldcrests. For many years, they were assumed to be spring and autumn migrants, of which just a few remained in the south of England for the winter, but about 40 years ago firecrests were discovered breeding in the New Forest and the Chilterns. Now firecrests are also found in coastal Suffolk, south-eastern Kent, Epping Forest in Essex, the Forest of Dean in Gloucestershire and on the Hampshire–Surrey border. It seems possible that firecrests may colonise new areas of conifers within mixed woodlands with open spaces. For the time being, however, numbers vary greatly from year to year. In good years there may be a 100 pairs or more, along with a few lone males that fail to find mates.

In the autumn, numbers may be swelled by some of these tiny birds being blown off course by high winds. In the second half of October, anticyclones probably drive them westwards, but the extent of the autumn and spring influx depends not only on the weather conditions at the time, but also on the population level of firecrests on the Continent. After a run of mild winters, numbers build up and the birds seem to become more mobile,

▲ A singing male firecrest splays out his golden yellow crest along with the black stripe that borders it. He often sings from the tops of tall trees.

although information on the movements of individual birds is speculative because of the lack of recoveries of ringed firecrests. At places such as Dungeness in Kent, however, they can be briefly common.

During the colder months, firecrests can be seen anywhere in the countryside as they roam about with flocks of goldcrests. When feeding together, the firecrest seems to forage lower down the tree than the goldcrest.

◄ Like goldcrests, firecrests are often secretive. Migrating birds may be tempted into gardens in southern Britain in autumn, when they often mix with tits.

The female begins to incubate the clutch before she has finished laying and so the chicks hatch at different times. There are so many eggs that she uses her legs and feet as well as her body to diffuse heat throughout the whole brood. Hatching takes 15–17 days, which is longer than for many similarly sized birds.

Birds' nests are normally at risk from predators, but the goldcrest's nest is so small and well concealed that the extra time the youngsters spend in it before fledging is not particularly risky for them. The male feeds the female at the nest and both parents provide food for the nestlings.

What is truly astonishing is that the birds start to build another nest for a second brood while still feeding the first batch of young. The female may be laying her second clutch and even, in some cases, incubating them before the first brood has flown the first nest. This

overlapping of broods is an amazing feat and extremely rare among British birds.

Survival through numbers

Goldcrests breed while the days are long and when maximum food is available. Although the invertebrates they eat are small, they are relatively large compared to the body size of the birds. The nest is well insulated so the eggs and nestlings are unlikely to lose heat quickly, which means that the odds for survival are stacked in their favour. During the summer, a pair raises 20 or so nestlings in their two broods.

There is an important reason for this productivity. These tiny birds are on the borderline of survival during cold winters. The smaller an animal, the larger its surface area compared to body weight and therefore the greater its potential for heat loss. In the depths of winter, the days are short and the nights long and cold. The birds must feed all day so as to build up energy for the night ahead, when roosting birds huddle together in thick cover to conserve heat.

Despite this, many goldcrests die during the course of a normal winter and even fewer survive an extremely cold one.

In April, the male goldcrest starts singing to claim a territory and attract a mate. The song is a rapidly repeated series of high-pitched but sweet-sounding phrases, which ends in a short, squeaky trill.

When a goldcrest is actively engaged in search of food, it can be hard to see its distinctive crest. However, when alarmed the bird may flash its crown.

After a run of particularly severe winters, numbers may be reduced by as much as 75 to 80 per cent but the birds' prolific breeding ability allows the species to survive and, if successive winters are mild, the population soon recovers.

New homes

Currently, goldcrest numbers seem to be increasing and this is probably partly due to the new coniferous forests that have been planted all over Britain and Ireland in recent years. In the tallest conifers, such as the big redwood grove in the Midlands, each breeding pair will remain within its own particular layer of the tree. This means that several territories can overlap, effectively stacked on top of each other. In such good habitats, careful plotting of the birds' territories has shown that there are often large areas with five or six pairs of goldcrests per hectare (2½ acres). Few other territorial birds reach anything like this breeding density in Britain.

From this angle, the goldcrest's comparatively short wings look broad and rounded, making the bird look like a miniature owl.

WILDLIFE WATCH

How can I see goldcrests and firecrests?

● Sit quietly in a conifer wood and listen for the goldcrest's high-pitched song (undetectable to people with hearing loss). The birds sing at almost any time of the year. Despite their natural wariness, goldcrests can become confident with humans and come quite close.

● Goldcrests may be seen in small groups. You can identify the sex of the birds if they confront each other and raise their crests – a flash of orange means that the bird is a male. However, if the crest is not raised, the flame centre is hidden, plus it is hard to see the crown from below.

● In the absence of coniferous woodland, try an old churchyard or garden with a big yew or cedar tree. Just one large yew is often enough to house a pair of goldcrests. The birds' thin bills enable them to feed on insects hidden between the needles.

● Firecrests are much rarer than their smaller cousins, and can be recognised by the black eyestripe. The bronze 'cloak' effect on the shoulders can sometimes be seen from below. Another clue is the slightly more insistent and tinny call. In winter, firecrests are quite likely to visit gardens in the company of goldcrests and may even take fat from hanging feeders.

The pheasant

Although it lives mostly on the ground, this exotic-looking bird prefers to roost in a tree. It has a distinctive way of taking off, rising almost vertically with a noisy beating of wings.

The pheasant has become a traditional and enduring element of the British countryside, despite being a native of China and south-east Asia. It is one of the large group of gamebirds – which includes partridges, quails, grouse, turkeys and guinea fowl – and is related to chickens. The various pheasant sub-species and hybrids include the predecessor of the domestic chicken (the red jungle fowl), as well as the crested argus pheasant – the males of which have in their tails the longest feathers of any wild birds – and ruffed species such as the golden and Lady Amherst's pheasants. This group, called the *Galliformes*, comprises the main gamebirds to be found across much of temperate Europe and North America.

Bred for the table

It is thought that the Greeks first imported pheasants to Europe from China as table birds, and that they may have been established in Britain as early as Roman times. However, the first evidence of pheasants breeding in the wild in Britain comes from a royal decree

▲ The plumage of the male, or cock, pheasant is variable but always colourful. The pheasant's success in Britain is partly the result of human nurturing and partly due to its ability to thrive on farmland that many other species cannot tolerate.

issued at the end of the 1400s granting their nests protection. From that time, they spread throughout the land, exploiting shrubby forest edges and farmland as well as their preferred reedbeds and other wetland vegetation, which is common in China.

Over the last century, pheasant numbers have increased due to the species' popularity as a gamebird. Gamekeepers incubate eggs, care for chicks and nurture large flocks. They prepare locations for the birds' benefit, remove their enemies and create opportunities for them to thrive. Around 20 million birds are reared annually and each season around 12 million are shot.

◄ The female, or hen, pheasant is generally smaller than the male, and lacks the fine glossy feathers that characterise the cock. She also lacks the prominent spurs found on the legs of the male.

PROTECTED!

The pheasant is protected by strict game laws. These include the provision of a shooting season, which lasts from 1 October to 1 February. Pheasant shooting is prohibited outside this period.

PHEASANT FACT FILE

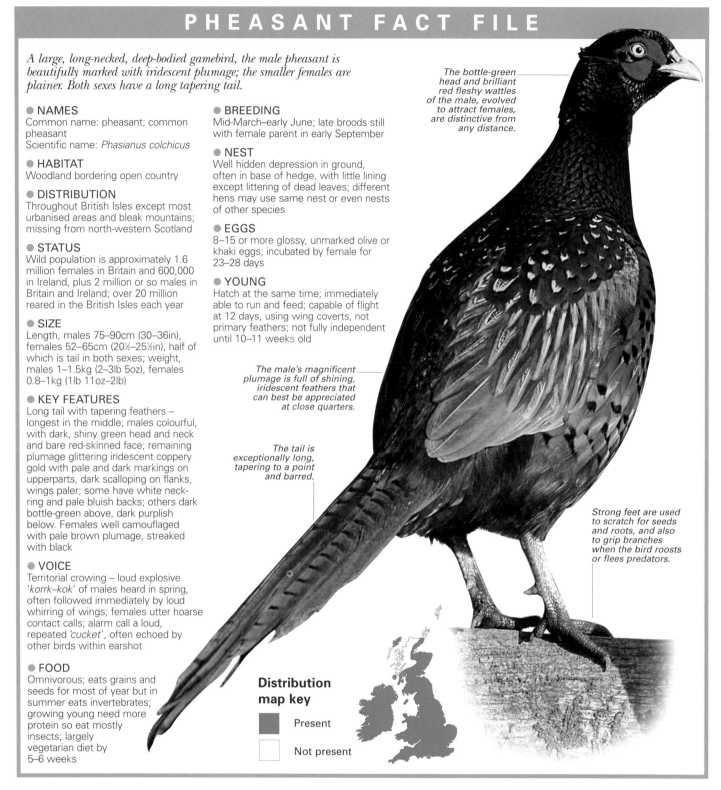

A large, long-necked, deep-bodied gamebird, the male pheasant is beautifully marked with iridescent plumage; the smaller females are plainer. Both sexes have a long tapering tail.

● NAMES
Common name: pheasant; common pheasant
Scientific name: *Phasianus colchicus*

● HABITAT
Woodland bordering open country

● DISTRIBUTION
Throughout British Isles except most urbanised areas and bleak mountains; missing from north-western Scotland

● STATUS
Wild population is approximately 1.6 million females in Britain and 600,000 in Ireland, plus 2 million or so males in Britain and Ireland; over 20 million reared in the British Isles each year

● SIZE
Length, males 75–90cm (30–36in), females 52–65cm (20½–25½in), half of which is tail in both sexes; weight, males 1–1.5kg (2–3lb 5oz), females 0.8–1kg (1lb 11oz–2lb)

● KEY FEATURES
Long tail with tapering feathers – longest in the middle; males colourful, with dark, shiny green head and neck and bare red-skinned face; remaining plumage glittering iridescent coppery gold with pale and dark markings on upperparts, dark scalloping on flanks, wings paler; some have white neck-ring and pale bluish backs; others dark bottle-green above, dark purplish below. Females well camouflaged with pale brown plumage, streaked with black

● VOICE
Territorial crowing – loud explosive '*korrk–kok*' of males heard in spring, often followed immediately by loud whirring of wings; females utter hoarse contact calls; alarm call a loud, repeated '*cucket*', often echoed by other birds within earshot

● FOOD
Omnivorous; eats grains and seeds for most of year but in summer eats invertebrates; growing young need more protein so eat mostly insects; largely vegetarian diet by 5–6 weeks

● BREEDING
Mid-March–early June; late broods still with female parent in early September

● NEST
Well hidden depression in ground, often in base of hedge, with little lining except littering of dead leaves; different hens may use same nest or even nests of other species

● EGGS
8–15 or more glossy, unmarked olive or khaki eggs; incubated by female for 23–28 days

● YOUNG
Hatch at the same time; immediately able to run and feed; capable of flight at 12 days, using wing coverts, not primary feathers; not fully independent until 10–11 weeks old

The bottle-green head and brilliant red fleshy wattles of the male, evolved to attract females, are distinctive from any distance.

The male's magnificent plumage is full of shining, iridescent feathers that can best be appreciated at close quarters.

The tail is exceptionally long, tapering to a point and barred.

Strong feet are used to scratch for seeds and roots, and also to grip branches when the bird roosts or flees predators.

Distribution map key

■ Present

□ Not present

Improved management

Pheasants favour wooded areas, but typical farmland with hedgerows makes an attractive alternative. Over much of the countryside, many features that are both pleasing to the eye and important to wildlife are there because landowners know their value in maintaining a good population of pheasants to shoot. There has been a serious loss of farmland hedges and woodlands over the last 40 years, and this would undoubtedly have been much worse without the pheasant as an inducement for their retention.

In the past, gamekeeping has been perceived negatively because of its impact on other wild animals. For example, pheasant-rearing pens used to be a focus of contention because owls and birds of prey were often attracted to the masses of young and apparently unprotected birds. Gamekeepers dedicated to preserving the safety of their small charges would dispatch these predators ruthlessly, shooting, snaring and poisoning them and hanging their carcasses on the notorious 'gamekeeper's gibbet'. The situation improved with the

legal protection of all birds of prey and owls. Today, rearing pens are not so crowded and are furnished with plenty of cover. Birds of prey such as buzzards, sparrowhawks and tawny owls may still take young pheasants, but the proportion has decreased dramatically.

Much of today's countryside management for pheasants involves the deliberate creation and maintenance of an environment that is also excellent for other wildlife. Scrubby coverts are ideal for many birds, such as turtle doves, linnets and willow warblers, and in

Scratching about

Pheasants are close relatives of the chicken and behave in similar ways. They spend most of their time on the ground, scratching with their strong scaly feet to turn up food in the form of insects or seeds.

In between inspecting the ground for food, male pheasants move by taking long strides – the bird maintains perfect poise using his long neck and tail as counterbalances.

▲ As spring gets warmer, males defend their territories with loud crowing, followed by a brief but vigorous flapping of wings. Such displays occur every 10 to 15 minutes at the peak of the season.

summer they become superb places for butterflies and moths. Of the greatest value to wildlife is managed woodland because it encourages resident birds, including tits and woodpeckers, as well as migrants, such as the blackcap and garden warbler. A wide variety of insects and mammals, especially foxes and small rodents, also flourish in the border areas created to provide cover for gamebirds.

Female harems

In spring, male pheasants are often outnumbered by females. In these circumstances, the cock may attract a harem of hens that follow him as he struts around. The harem may number anything from two to ten or more. The highest number of hens recorded in one harem is 18.

PHEASANT YOUNG

Pheasants nest on the ground, often starting quite early in the year. The female chooses somewhere under cover of a bush or hedge, in long grass. The nest is a bed of grassy material, and the eggs have a very smooth, almost glossy shell. They are a pale khaki or olive with no markings and are relatively rounded.

The female incubates the eggs for more than three weeks, seldom leaving the nest. The chicks hatch almost simultaneously and scatter from the nest to hide in the surrounding vegetation. They have a dense covering of buff-coloured down, marked with

blotches and streaks of brown, which provides good camouflage – extremely important in a ground-nesting species. Their flight feathers grow later.

◄ A pheasant's nest can hold as many as 17 eggs. Sometimes this may be due to many birds living in one area, which encourages several females to lay in the same nest.

▲ The tiny chicks are remarkably precocious from birth, being able to run around, feed themselves and later to fly at less than two weeks old. Their mother cares for them for up to 80 days.

While the hens are feeding as much as they can in order to prepare for egg laying and looking after young, the cock stands guard and defends them from any marauding males, while hopefully attracting more females to his troop. The hens mainly feed at dawn and dusk, usually in arable fields on sprouting crops, and then return to the woods,

where the open cover of a woodland glade enables the male to continue to keep a possessive eye on them.

Road danger

Few birds seem to be more prone to disaster on the roads than pheasants. Along many country lanes and even motorways, as many as five pheasant bodies may lie on the roadside every couple of kilometres at certain times of the year, but this apparently suicidal tendency is the result of quite natural behaviour. If woodland glades for the birds to retreat to after feeding are few and far between, roadside verges make good substitutes. For this reason, breeding birds may be attracted to roadsides and so spend much of their time in an area where they risk being killed by traffic.

Later on, young, inexperienced birds are especially vulnerable, and if a group is split on either side of the road, those on one side might suddenly dart back across the road to try to join the others.

Unsociable males

While the hens are rearing the young, the males spend the summer patrolling grain fields in groups of two or three. They prefer to stay near a tree or some other safe haven that they can fly to if they feel threatened, climbing almost vertically into the air as they take off.

When the crops are cut in the autumn, all the pheasants move back to the woods. The males spread out to establish their own territories and they compete fiercely for the best places. If the wood is small, those males that find themselves lower down in the pecking order may move out to nearby hedgerows or bushes. The females are much more gregarious and less aggressive, forming flocks and spending the winter together in the security of the wood.

Nature's oddities

The spread of pheasants has been due mainly to birds being reared and released by humans, and during this process a number of mutations have emerged.

PHEASANT CALENDAR

JANUARY • FEBRUARY

The breeding season starts as early as late January. Crowing cocks noisily display their beautiful plumage to impress females. Where sex ratios are near even, pairs will form rather than harems.

MARCH • APRIL

Egg laying can start as early as late March in warm and mild springs, but most nests are only just being built at this time. Eggs start to be laid in mid-April at the rate of one per day.

MAY • JUNE

Incubation begins in May and the first tiny chicks appear from mid-May onwards. Many are lost to predators and the weather, so re-nesting attempts will carry on throughout May and well into June.

JULY • AUGUST

Females and chicks stay together for six weeks or more. The earliest chicks are usually fully grown by late August. The female is a good mother, but the males seldom take any part in rearing the young.

SEPTEMBER • OCTOBER

The first day of October heralds the start of the legal shooting season. Males are approaching their prime and take to the air with a sudden explosion of beating wings as they are flushed from cover.

NOVEMBER • DECEMBER

As winter hardens, male pheasants tend to remain alone whereas females will form flocks of between five and 30 birds loosely grouped together, the composition of which continually changes.

◄ **The male's facial wattles and ear-like tufts will swell and become erect during his courtship display. These shows are designed to display their exotic shining plumage in its full glory.**

►**The chestnut plumage of the male's back shows a scalloped pattern with bold black markings on each feather.**

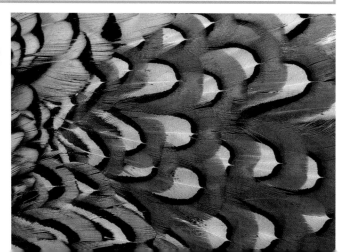

This partly melanistic cock could be the result of a mutation or a cross with another species. The neck and underparts are glossy purple-blue, the rest mainly olive-brown.

The most common is the black, or melanistic, pheasant. These handsome birds occur wherever pheasants are found but they are particularly common in Britain where they have been encouraged by gamekeepers. The males are very dark, with their under-feather colouring a deep matt black. The visible parts of the feathers are deep purple or blue-green and the birds hardly ever have a white neck-ring. The hens are particularly noticeable as they are a uniform chocolate brown.

Other plumage variants include white birds, which are not true albinos as the males still have pigmented red wattles, or facial skin flaps, and 'Bohemian' birds, which have white under-feathers and pale colours and markings at the feather tips.

RUFFED PHEASANTS

The common pheasant is not the only pheasant species to breed in the wild in Britain. Two others are spectacular ruffed birds – the golden pheasant and Lady Amherst's pheasant. Originally from the forests of the Far East, the cocks of both species are gloriously coloured with exceptionally long tails.

The golden pheasant cock has a gold head, throat, neck and mantle, with red plumes, brilliant orange and black ear-tufts and a bright red breast and underparts. Its tail is mainly black and flecked with small white spots.

The tail of the cock Lady Amherst's pheasant is white, flecked and barred with black. It has a crimson crest, grey face, dark green throat, breast and wing coverts and striking white ear coverts with black

The Lady Amherst's pheasant was first introduced in the 1890s and has become established in a small area of the south. A secretive bird, it is often difficult to spot despite its conspicuous appearance.

terminal crescents. Both birds are difficult to see because, although they have striking plumage, they usually skulk in the deep shade of woodland undergrowth. They are most often heard in the breeding season when the males utter loud, piercing single or double syllable 'tchack' cries.

The two species are closely related and the birds in Britain may include hybrids. Golden

◀ In parts of Britain, enough golden pheasants have been released to form seemingly stable wild populations. These are thought to be the only viable non-captive populations outside China.

pheasants are most common around the Brecklands of Suffolk and Norfolk, the South Downs of Hampshire and Sussex and Galloway Forest Park, Scotland, but they are declining in numbers and range. There may be only around a thousand of these birds left in Britain.

Lady Amherst's are far rarer and the only well established population is around Woburn in Bedfordshire, where they were originally released about a hundred years ago. The total British population is fewer than a hundred birds.

There have been various releases and escapes of other species in Britain. The Reeve's pheasant, from northern China where it is now rare, existed for 20 or 30 years in the Scottish Highlands but, despite further introductions, is thought to have died out there. The males are striking birds, having white heads with a broad dark mask and burnished bronze plumage with dark terminal marks and a very long tail.

The nearest completely wild populations of the common pheasant are those around the eastern shores of the Black Sea. These pheasants do not have the white ring round the neck that characterises the familiar semi-nurtured breed.

Many other sub-species can be found naturally across Asia to its Pacific coast; the ones with the most white in their collars come from Mongolia.

A closely related species, the green pheasant, has been introduced in some areas and sometimes interbreeds with the common British species.

Masculine disguise

Another unusual form that occurs with surprising frequency is the mule. These birds, although female, develop varying amounts of male plumage. In Britain, they probably account for about 1 hen in 500. Mules, or gynandromorphs as they are correctly known, have the blue head, bronzed body and, on occasion, the neck-ring of the male. A closer look, however, reveals that they have no proper wattles, ear-tufts or spurs, and the tail is short and plain like a true female.

Mules are not born this way. Their condition usually results from damage to the ovaries, such as avian tuberculosis, which causes them to stop producing the right balance of female hormones. In pheasants this imbalance leads to 'maleness' in terms of general plumage, although a lack of the male hormone testosterone prevents them from acquiring a full complement of male features, such as spurs, ear-tufts, wattles and the spectacular tail. Moreover, mules continue to act like females, laying and incubating eggs, and caring for chicks. Mules are probably responsible for reports of males seen performing such female duties.

DID YOU KNOW?

The largest number of pheasants shot in a single day was the 3,937 bagged by King George V and six other shooters (including the future Edward VIII) in Buckinghamshire in 1913. Despite slaughter on such a huge scale, pheasants remain among the most abundant birds in the British Isles.

Mutations such as this white male are relatively common in some areas, especially where birds are artificially reared. In more natural conditions, such distinctive birds would be singled out easily by predators.

Sitting pretty

Hen pheasants are well camouflaged, whether sitting quietly on their nests or feeding sociably amid long grass and weeds in meadows and hedgerows.

Female pheasants peck nervously, stopping every few seconds to listen for danger. Hens are more sociable than males, in the winter often forming groups of up to 30 birds.

WILDLIFE WATCH

Where can I see pheasants?

● Pheasants are very common throughout lowland Britain and Ireland, often thanks to active assistance by gamekeepers. Protection of wild birds is achieved through controlling their predators and supplementary feeding. The rearing and release of huge quantities of young pheasants each year maintains their numbers.

● Groups of females, often up to ten, with their attendant cock bird, may be seen in open areas in spring. During spring and summer, the birds are often to be found near roadside verges where they are frequent victims of traffic. To avoid collision (and possibly a bill for repairs) be prepared to slow down and flash your headlights to attract the birds' attention and encourage them to move off the road.

● Many birdwatchers do not pay much attention to pheasants because they are common birds, mostly artificially reared and released. However, the birds are individually very variable and it is well worth studying the male's plumage carefully. One common difference is the presence or lack of a white ring round the neck. Also, look out for very dark birds or white ones, and female birds with varying levels of male plumage.

● In many rural areas, pheasants regularly feed in nearby gardens and get to know in which ones they are likely to find food. In such cases, they often show themselves readily and fearlessly.

Woodlice

Armour-plated woodlice come out to feed at night among fallen leaves and decaying plants. During the day, they lie low under logs and stones, and scurry for cover if disturbed.

The shady underside of almost any stone or fallen log provides a suitable place for woodlice to hide. Easily recognised as a group by their flattened and segmented bodies, these little invertebrates are Britain's only terrestrial crustaceans, members of the order Isopoda – a group usually associated with watery locations. Worldwide, there are 3500 or so species of woodlice. Their marine and freshwater relatives include sea slaters (or water 'lice'), crabs and lobsters.

Although they may not be entirely at home on dry land – most are restricted to damp locations – woodlice are often present in huge numbers. Like all crustaceans, as well as insects, spiders, centipedes and millipedes, woodlice are arthropods – invertebrates with jointed legs and generally a hard outer covering,

▲ Leaf litter is a rich hunting ground for the common woodlouse, *Oniscus asellus*. This is one of the most regularly encountered species of woodlouse and its diet comprises mainly leaf mould.

▶ *Cylisticus convexus* is scarcer than the common woodlouse. It is one of the few species that, when under threat, will curl up into an armour-plated ball, leaving just its antennae waving in the air.

or exoskeleton. Armoured plates called tergites protect the woodlouse's soft body from damage. Its body, around 15mm (⅝in) long, is divided into three broad segments – the head, thorax and abdomen.

In common with other crustaceans, leg-like appendages grow from each body segment. These 'legs' have the same basic structure but their functions vary greatly.

▲ *Platyarthus hoffmannseggi* is a tiny white blind woodlouse found only in the nests of ants, mainly the yellow ant *Lasius flavus*. The ants take no notice of these lodgers.

▲ After mating, young woodlice develop inside eggs carried around in the mother's brood pouch. Once hatched, they remain in the pouch for a few days and will cling to the mother's body when they emerge.

Most of them are adapted for walking, but some act as sensory antennae while others work as external gills and, in male woodlice, the first two pairs are external sex organs.

Woodlice mate after dark and under cover. The male climbs on to the female's back and inseminates her using his front 'legs'. The eggs develop inside a pouch on the underside of the female's body and, after a month or so, tiny replicas of the adults hatch. The young take two years to mature and woodlice usually live for two to four years.

Nocturnal feeding

Unlike insects and spiders, woodlice have no waxy cuticles to prevent water loss, so they can dry out and die in just a few hours. They come out to feed only on damp days or at night, when humidity is high and darkness hides them from predatory birds. This does not prevent them being eaten by nocturnal hunters – woodlice are on the menu for shrews, hedgehogs, toads, frogs, newts and a

specialist spider, *Dysdera crocata*, that is equipped with proportionately huge fangs for puncturing their shells.

Daylight hours are spent hidden beneath stones or logs or in crevices in the ground. Woodlice are, by and large, solitary creatures, but good hideaways can be in short supply, so crowds of woodlice may gather in safe, humid locations. One species likes the company of different invertebrates. *Platyarthus hoffmannseggi* lives among colonies of ants, where it feeds on the faeces of its hosts.

Woodlice do not do any serious damage to plants. Many of them are scavengers and feed on soft plant leaves, fungi and decaying plant material, such as dead wood, effectively recycling the nutrients. They also eat their own droppings in order to resorb moisture and get the most from their food.

▲ A close look at a pill woodlouse (*Armadillidium vulgare*) reveals how it got its name. With little provocation, it will curl into a tight ball, its scales overlapping to protect the soft, vulnerable underparts.

THE SEA SLATER

Terrestrial woodlice evolved from marine crustaceans via an intermediate form that probably looked very much like sea slaters. Although they live on land, breathing air, these woodlouse relatives are seldom found more than a few metres from the sea and are perfectly able to tolerate being submerged under sea

water. They prefer to remain out of sight for much of the time and hide in crevices, beneath rocks and among seaweed debris around the high-tide mark.

The best way to find a sea slater, is to turn over stones and boulders on a rocky shore. However, unlike their terrestrial cousins, sea slaters can move back under cover at quite a pace. An even better strategy for discovering sea slaters is to venture on to the shore after dark and look for them using a torch.

Although about 50 species of sea slater are included among British woodlice, fewer than ten could be described as common.

◄ By woodlouse standards, the sea slater is a large and active creature. It forages on the shoreline, feeding on organic debris – mostly seaweeds – washed up on to the beach by waves.

WILDLIFE WATCH

Where can I find woodlice?

● Most gardens shelter plenty of woodlice. Search beneath the stones in a rockery, among log piles or in leaf litter and compost, or lift up flower pots on a patio. Woodlice eat mainly organic detritus, and so provide a valuable recycling service to gardeners. They do no damage to garden furniture.

● In woodland, look under the bark of fallen logs or turn over the logs themselves. Always remember to turn a log back again once you have finished, thereby restoring the animals' safe haven.

● The seashore can be a surprisingly good place for woodlice. The related sea slater lives on rocky shores while several scarce species are found on the strand line of shingle beaches.

Plant galls

Oak apples and robin's pincushions are just two of a number of galls to be found growing on trees and shrubs. These weird swellings are as varied as the organisms that cause them – from bacteria and fungi to wasps and midges.

Bizarrely distorted acorns developing on an oak tree in early autumn are among the most conspicuous examples of the unusual and abnormal growths known as plant galls. These growths – caused by insects or other organisms invading the plant's tissues – provide the attacker with both food and shelter. Any part of a plant, from roots to seeds, may be affected, although each gall-causing organism usually attacks just one area of the plant.

Oak apples, visible from late spring, and in summer robin's pincushions (bedeguar galls) are also obvious, but many galls are tiny and some are completely hidden within the host plant. Some galls take the form of clearly swollen or modified stems or buds; others, including the various spangle galls on oaks and bean galls on willows, are totally new structures, separate from the normal growth of the plant.

Plant invaders

Plant galls are induced by a wide variety of organisms, including bacteria, fungi and nematode worms, but the great majority are caused by insects and mites. Among the insects, the two main gall-causing groups are the gall wasps and a collection of tiny flies known as gall

▶ Robin's pincushions are among the more attractive plant galls. They are commonly found on wild roses and are formed when the gall wasp *Diplolepis rosae* lays eggs in a flower bud.

▲ A section through a robin's pincushion reveals several dozen white grubs inside. The normal development of the flower bud is disrupted by chemicals secreted by the female laying the eggs and by the grubs themselves.

DID YOU KNOW?

The study of galls is called cecidology from the Greek word *kekis* for a gall. Over 2000 different kinds of plant galls have so far been discovered in the British Isles, and it seems likely that many more await discovery.

The insects that cause gall growth benefit from the relationship with the plant because food and shelter is provided for their larvae. However, it is not so easy to see what a plant stands to gain from allowing its tissues to be co-opted by the gall-makers. A lot of food material is diverted to the galls for the use of the developing inhabitants and, if flowers or fruits are attacked, the reproductive potential of the plants is diminished. In spite of all this, the host plants do not seem unduly inconvenienced by galls. A single oak leaf can carry more than 100 spangle galls and, even if thousands of leaves are affected in this way, the tree does not seem to suffer.

It is possible that gall formation evolved as the plants' way of restricting damage by insects and other creatures. By growing specialist structures to enclose the parasites and provide them with everything they need, the plant can protect its more vital tissues from unwanted invasion.

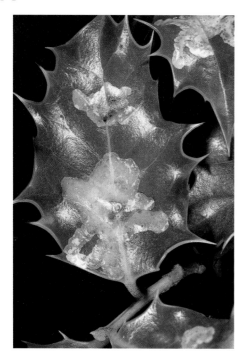

▲ The holly leaf miner is the larva of the gall fly *Phytomyza ilicis*. The colourless tracks on the surface of the leaf show the progress of the larva as it munches its way around the confined space within the leaf.

▲ Spangle galls are caused by gall wasps, females of which lay eggs in clusters on the leaves. A single larva develops inside each gall. The galls then drop off the leaf in autumn, allowing the grub to overwinter in leaf litter on the ground.

▶ Marble galls are much harder than the leaf tissues from which they grow. They also contain tannin, which may deter other insects from attacking the nutritious tissues and defenceless grubs within.

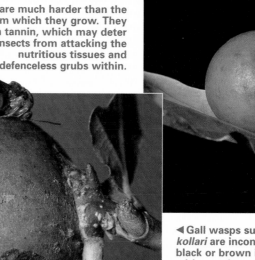

◀ Gall wasps such as *Andricus kollari* are inconspicuous-looking black or brown insects, with or without wings. Indeed, they actually look more like ants than typical wasps.

midges. Aphids, psyllids, sawflies and weevils can also cause galls. Although gall formation is stimulated by the invading organisms, galls themselves always consist entirely of plant cells.

The formation of galls depends on the plants' reactions to chemicals released by the invaders. Most insect-induced galls develop in response to some substance in the saliva of the feeding larvae. Whatever the nature of the chemical stimuli, they cause the surrounding plant cells to enlarge and multiply rapidly. The gall tissues are particularly nutritious for the gall-causers that feed on them.

Each gall-causing species induces its own kind of gall because each uses a specific chemical stimulus to influence the tissues of the host plant in a particular way. Two closely related gall-causers can generate two different kinds of gall. Take, for example, two gall wasps *Neuroterus quercusbaccarum* and *N. numismalis*. The wasps are very alike – both target oak leaves in the summer – but *N. quercusbaccarum* is responsible for the common spangle gall and *N. numismalis*, the silk button spangle gall.

Wasp effects

Gall wasps belong to the family *Cynipidae* and are distantly related to the more familiar black-and-yellow wasps. About 90 species live in the British Isles, although not all of them induce galls – quite a number live as guests in the galls of other species. Gall wasps are responsible for robin's pincushions and 'sputnik' galls on

roses, and for cigar-like swellings in the stems of brambles, but most are associated with oaks. Oak apples, marble galls, artichoke galls, cherry galls and the various spangle galls are all induced by gall wasps. Some contain a single insect within one chamber (unilocular galls); others house several wasps in several chambers (plurilocular galls).

Many gall wasps, especially those associated with oaks, have complicated life cycles involving alternate sexual and asexual generations. Insects of the sexual generation include males and females, which mate and lay eggs in the normal way. The asexual generation consists

entirely of females that lay fertile eggs without mating. The generations usually cause markedly different galls. The sexual generation of *N. quercusbaccarum*, for example, grows in currant galls, which resemble redcurrants attached to oak catkins or leaves in May and June. The asexual generation, however, develops in the spangle galls that are so common on the undersides of the autumn leaves.

▶ Swollen bramble stems are a sign that the plant has been attacked by gall wasps. The culprits in this case have long gone, leaving telltale holes where the newly hatched insects bored their way out of the stem.

WITCHES' BROOMS

Witches' broom galls occur on a variety of trees, although they seem particularly common on birch and hornbeam. They are usually caused by fungi and consist of dense clusters of stunted twigs sprouting from a swollen region of a branch. They survive for many years and some reach a metre (3ft) or more in diameter.

◀ In summer, the sprouting twigs of the witches' broom gall are covered in leaves. When the leaves fall in late autumn and winter, the aptness of the name becomes apparent.

▶ Artichoke galls on yew branches are formed from truncated shoots in which the leaves grow very close together. The gall-causing insect is a tiny midge called *Taxomyia taxi,* after the yew *Taxus baccatum.*

The sexual generation of the wasp *Biorhiza pallida* develops in oak apples in spring and summer and usually emerges in June or July; the asexual generation develops in much smaller galls on young, slender oak roots. The two generations also look different – those emerging from the oak apples all have wings but the asexual insects, which emerge the following winter, are all wingless.

Males are extremely rare in some gall wasp species. For example, they account for only about 4 per cent of the population of *Diplolepis rosae,* which is responsible for the robin's pincushion gall. The females go on laying fertile eggs for generation after generation without ever mating.

Knopper galls, which form irregular, sticky caps on acorns, were unknown in the British Isles until the 1960s, but they are now common throughout England and Wales. They are caused by the asexual generation of the gall wasp *Andricus quercuscalicis,* which is one of several species that have recently arrived from the Continent. The larva lives in an inner chamber deep inside the acorn, which is

usually completely destroyed. The sexual generation of this species causes tiny galls on the catkins of the Turkey oak.

Knopper galls caused a certain amount of panic when they first appeared in Britain because many people thought they would destroy the oak population, but these fears have proved unfounded.

Aphid architecture

Although many aphids cause distortion of their host plants, relatively few cause galls. Most of the galls they do generate are little more than apparently crinkled leaves, with the aphids living in little domes or pouches that bubble up between the veins. The red blotches on redcurrant leaves, caused by *Cryptomyzus ribis,* are good examples of these simple galls. Elm leaves galled by *Eriosoma ulmi* form cigar-like tubes, but are still obviously modified leaves. The 'pineapple galls' caused by *Adelges* on spruce twigs are clearly stunted shoots, in which the leaf bases are swollen and tightly clustered together. *Pemphigus spyrothecae* causes poplar leaf stalks to coil up and enclose the aphids, but the very similar *P. bursarius*

induces a totally new structure in the form of a purse-like swelling on the leaf stalk. *Tetraneura ulmi* also induces purse-like galls on elm leaves.

Unlike the galls of flies and gall wasps, those of the aphids always have openings through which the insects can eject their wax-coated packets of honeydew.

Gall-causing flies

The midges of the family *Cecidomyiidae* – the ones that swarm around lights at night – are the most numerous of the gall-causing flies. Many have orange bodies and tiny wings with hardly any veins. They produce a range of galls on woody and herbaceous plants; opening the galls will reveal white, yellow or orange larvae.

▼ Aspen leaves are subject to invasion by the gall midge *Harmandia globuli.* The tiny midge larvae develop inside deep pink swellings on the surface of the leaves, feeding on the plant's cells.

◀ A knopper gall destroys the acorn from which it grows, but an oak tree can produce thousands of acorns in a season, so the galls are no real threat. In fact, the knopper gall is less abundant now than it was 20 years ago.

◀ Numerous young mites live inside each lighthouse gall. They are able to exit via openings on the underside of the leaf, although these openings are usually concealed by tufts of hair.

▶ The gall midge *Urophora cardui* causes hard swellings in the stems of thistles that are sometimes as big as a chicken's egg. This gall is quite common in the southern half of England and Wales.

Clusters of distorted leaves, which are usually abundant at the tips of hedgerow hawthorn shoots, are the galls of *Dasineura crataegi*, while dogwoods in the south of England often bear the neat, flask-shaped galls of *Craneiobia corni*. Germander speedwell is attacked by *Jaapiella veronicae*, which is responsible for the swollen, hairy tips of many of the shoots. Violets rarely escape the attentions of *Dasineura violae*, which causes swollen and distorted leaves, to the annoyance of many gardeners. However, not all galls are unsightly. The well-named 'lighthouse galls' of *Rondaniola bursaria*, which inhabit

the leaves of ground ivy, mature from green to red and are very attractive when studied through a magnifying lens.

Thistles and knapweeds are galled by several flies of the family *Tephritidae*, often called picture-winged flies because of their patterned wings. Most of these flies attack the fruits and their galls are not easily found, but *Urophora cardui* lives in the stems of creeping thistle.

The most familiar sawfly galls are red bean galls caused by *Pontania proxima* on willow leaves. Up to the size of a haricot bean, they protrude from both sides of the leaf blade and are usually red, although the underside is sometimes yellow or green. These galls begin to develop as soon as the female sawflies lay their eggs in the leaves, triggered by some chemical stimulus injected with the eggs, but they do not develop fully without the presence of feeding larvae. Each gall contains a single larva, which bites a small hole in the bottom of the gall through which it can eject its droppings.

Miniature galls

Most gall-causing mites belong to the family *Eriophyidae* and are rarely more than a tenth of a millimetre long. They

are sap feeders and the galls develop in response to the chemicals they inject into the plants' cells while feeding. Most of the galls appear as tiny pimples on the leaves of various plants, although not all such nodules are caused by mites – many gall midges generate similar pimple-like galls. The most familiar of the mite galls are the red pimples found on sycamore and maple leaves, the pink pustules around the edges of blackthorn leaves and the somewhat larger nail galls on lime leaves.

▶ Each silk button spangle gall contains a single developing wasp grub.

▼ The female gall wasp *Neuroterus numismalis* lays eggs on oak leaves in summer, leading to the development of silk button spangle galls.

Recognising woodland fungi

Displaying an astonishing array of shapes and sizes, these curious organisms push through the dead leaves of the woodland floor or sprout from the decaying trunks of fallen trees.

Fungi spend most of their lives as a mass of minute thread-like strands, called hyphae, hidden in the soil, in or among the roots of trees, or in dead wood. Here they play a part in the process of decay, helping to rot leaf mould, carcasses and any other organic matter that reaches the ground. In doing so, they help release vital chemicals back into the soil. Without fungi, woodland would soon be knee-deep in detritus.

The mushrooms or toadstools that seem to appear suddenly on warm, damp autumn days are the 'fruits' of the fungi, and these have one purpose – to ripen and release spores to form the next generation. Many last a few days, some just a matter of hours. Tougher, woody types, such as bracket fungi, can last for a month or more.

Different shapes

The fruits of most woodland fungi are shaped like umbrellas, but others are more like trumpets, ears or coral. Some look like pebbles, cauliflower, rice pudding, orange peel and even tiny hedgehogs. Each of these extraordinary forms has evolved to release as many spores as possible, as efficiently as possible. From the umbrella shape, the spores simply fall off into the air, aided by a little puff from the fungus. A heftier puff is needed to propel spores into the air from ear or bowl-shapes, and some fungi contain the equivalent of tiny water pistols, which shoot out spores explosively one at a time through a narrow aperture.

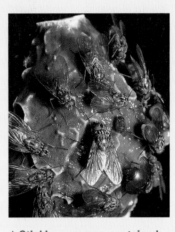

▲ Stinkhorn spores, contained in slimy, foul-smelling fluid, are lapped up by flies and dispersed in their droppings within a day of the fungus's appearance.

Inkcaps drop their spores in liquid and dissolve in the process, while the spores of bracket fungi, which grow on trees above the ground to start with, just drift out through a honeycomb of pores.

Woodland supports more fungi than any other habitat. The cool moist air beneath the branches is ideally suited to these organisms and decomposing leaves produce plenty of food for them.

▼ Fly agaric toadstools, with their scarlet caps speckled with white, are a magical sight, but don't touch because they are poisonous.

DANGER!

Many edible species of fungi have poisonous counterparts that look very similar. It can be extremely difficult to tell them apart. The best advice is not to collect fungi from the wild at all; otherwise, the golden rule is if in doubt about a specimen's identity, do not eat it. As a further word of warning, some species cause stomach upsets when consumed with alcohol.

EASY GUIDE TO SPOTTING WOODLAND FUNGI

WHAT ARE WOODLAND FUNGI?

● Most woodland fungi belong to the class Ascomycota or the class Basidiomycota. The spores of the ascomycetes develop within microscopic flask-shaped structures, called asci, that develop inside the fruiting body, usually in groups of eight. Those of the basidiomycetes develop on the outside of a club-like structure, called a basidium, usually in groups of four.

● The ascomycetes are varied in appearance, including star and cup shapes, the brain-like morels and the subterranean, tuber-like truffles.

● Many basidiomycetes have a cap and stalk. Among such mushroom-type forms, russulas and agarics have gills arranged in a radiating pattern on the underside of the cap, and agarics have a ring, or velum, surrounding the stalk near the top. Basidiomycetes that have no gills include the mushroom-like boletes and the bracket fungi, which resemble irregular shelves projecting from trunks and branches of mature upright or fallen trees. These fungi bear their spores in tubes opening through pores. Earth-stars, earthballs, phallus-shaped stinkhorns and bird's nest fungi complete with miniature 'eggs', have spore-bearing tissue enclosed within a sac that ruptures to release the spores. A separate, smallish group of basidiomycetes, known as jelly fungi, have a jelly-like feel except in dry conditions when they harden and shrivel, until rain moistens them.

HOW CAN I IDENTIFY WOODLAND FUNGI?

● Key features are the shape, colour and texture of the cap, stalk and ring, if present. The texture of the flesh when the fruiting body is cut in half differs between fungi, too, as do the colour, spacing and texture of the gills, and sometimes the odour. Remove the cap and leave it upside down on a piece of white paper overnight to make a spore-print and check the spore colour. Time of fruiting can be helpful but some species grow at any time of year when conditions are favourable.

● Cep, chanterelle and fly agaric live in association with tree roots, with which they exchange nutrients. Some fungi grow with particular trees, so different species may be found in a birch wood from those in beech or pine woods. Some grow on a particular type of tree in one part of the country and a different type elsewhere, and they may be found in different locations each year.

● Individuals of the same species can vary considerably, particularly between young and old specimens. Looking for a typical mature form and then becoming familiar with age variations will increase the chances of making correct identifications.

Honey fungus

Wood blewit

Chanterelle

Horn of plenty

Fly agaric

Charcoal burner

Death cap

Wood mushroom

The blusher

Saffron milkcap

Cep or penny bun

Stinkhorn

WILDLIFE WATCH

Where can I see woodland fungi?

● Look for hollow trees and stumps and half-buried branches and twigs. About a third of woodland fungi depend on dead wood for food.

● Mature beech trees, oaks, birches and Scots pines support many different species of fungi. Non-native trees such as horse chestnut and sitka spruce have very few.

● Some fungi occur only where special conditions are satisfied, such as on the burned ground of bonfire sites, on piles of wet sawdust or in boggy hollows with *Sphagnum* moss. The best places are often mossy banks at the edge of a wood where earth is exposed between shifting piles of dead leaves. The mass of fungus and tree roots, called a mycorrhiza, may occasionally be seen, when the roots are exposed.

HONEY FUNGUS *Armillaria mellea*

The stems of this large agaric fungus fuse at the base as dense clusters grow at the foot of trees and on stumps. The cap may be flat, domed or funnel shaped, and such is the variation in shape and colour that the name may cover a group of very closely related species.

When honey fungi attack a living tree, the tree invariably dies, creating niches for animals to live in the rotting wood.

● SIZE
Cap 8–9cm (3–3½in) wide; stem 10–15cm (4–6in) high

● KEY FEATURES
Colour varies from honey-brown to yellow or olive; cap slightly scaly; gills white, becoming spotted with brown; stem same colour as cap and bears pale ring. Grows in sizeable clumps

● SEASON
Fruits mainly from September to November

● HABITAT
Parasitic at the base of living trees, but also grows on dead stumps and on partly buried timber

● DISTRIBUTION
Widespread on broad-leaved trees, especially oak and beech

WOOD BLEWIT *Lepista nuda*

A medium-sized agaric that often grows in groups or rings, the wood blewit is among those fungi that continue to produce fruiting bodies after the first frosts of early winter. As with many other species, the caps of these fungi often become damaged by maggots as they age.

The distinctive pinkish and violet colours of the cap, gills and stem make this fungus relatively easy to identify.

● SIZE
Cap 5–15cm (2–6in) wide, stem 5–20cm (2–8in) high

● KEY FEATURES
Violet gills with flattish violet-brown or pinkish cap and fibrous deep lilac-purple stem (white near top) that turns browner with maturity. Has a pleasant smell of aniseed

● SEASON
Fruits in late autumn, before first frosts

● HABITAT
Woodland tracksides and banks and among leaf litter

● DISTRIBUTION
Widespread, occurring in both broad-leaved and coniferous woodlands

CHANTERELLE *Cantharellus cibarius*

One of a group of basidiomycetes classified in the order Cantharellales, the chanterelle has shallow folds in place of proper gills. It is edible but may be confused with several other woodland species that have true gills and are poisonous.

Although brightly coloured, the chanterelle can be easily overlooked on dull days since it often grows in deep shade.

● SIZE
Cap 2–10cm (¾–4in) wide; stem 2–10cm (¾–4in) high

● KEY FEATURES
Deep yellow trumpet-shaped fungus, often tinged orange or brown; cap has wavy edge and often has a slight hollow at the centre; shallow folds in place of true gills. Smells pleasantly of dried apricots

● SEASON
Fruits from August to early October

● HABITAT
Sandy or chalky soil, especially under pines and spruce, but also quite often encountered beneath beech, birch and oak

● DISTRIBUTION
Widespread, may be common in places

HORN OF PLENTY *Craterellus cornucopioides*

Classified in the same order as the chanterelles, the alternative name for this fungus is the black trumpet. In France it is known as *trompette de mort*, 'trumpet of death', although it is not poisonous. It has no gills. The spore-producing layer on the outer surface is ash-grey and wrinkles with age.

The sombre horn of plenty may be found among the dead leaves of the woodland floor.

● SIZE
Cap 3–8cm (1¼–3in) wide, stem 5–12cm (2–4¾in) high

● KEY FEATURES
Thin-fleshed, completely hollow trumpets, usually occurring in large numbers, almost black inside fading to greyish brown with age; stem often covered with white dusting of spores

● SEASON
Fruits from late summer all through the autumn

● HABITAT
Broad-leaved woods on rich alkaline soil, often under beech; moss and dead leaves, often on clay banks

● DISTRIBUTION
Patchy; usually grows in clusters or 'troops'

FLY AGARIC *Amanita muscaria*

When this large poisonous agaric first appears above ground, its scarlet cap and white stem are enclosed in a knobbly white veil, the remains of which form the spots on the cap, the ring on the stem and the volva (membranous sac) at its base. Concoctions of this fungus were used to kill flies.

Groups of fly agarics vary in age and size, from miniature young domes to mature spreading giants.

- **SIZE**
Cap 6–15cm (2½–6in) or more; stem 8–20cm (3–8in) high

- **KEY FEATURES**
Red cap with white 'spots' – actually scales of tissue; cap fades to orange or yellowish with age. Contains toxin muscarine, which, if ingested, causes sickness, diarrhoea and hallucinations and can be fatal

- **SEASON**
Fruits from summer to late autumn

- **HABITAT**
Under birch trees in grass and bracken; less commonly under pine and spruce

- **DISTRIBUTION**
Widespread; very common in places, occurring in 'troops' or sometimes in rings

THE BLUSHER *Amanita rubescens*

If rubbed or broken, in hot or rainy weather, or when nibbled by slugs, the flesh of this large poisonous toadstool becomes mottled pinkish, turning brown in time – a characteristic reflected in the species' common name. The warty patches on the cap may be dense or sparse.

As with other species of *Amanita*, the pale flecks on the cap may be washed off by heavy rain.

- **SIZE**
Cap 6–15cm (2½–6in) wide; stem 6–15cm (2½–6in) high

- **KEY FEATURES**
Rounded, flesh-coloured cap with pale or reddish warty patches; reddens with age; stout stem is white to pinkish grey; large ring white or pinkish to yellow; swollen, conical base

- **SEASON**
Fruits from late summer through the autumn, peaking late August to early September

- **HABITAT**
All types of woodland, especially birch, oak, beech, pine and spruce on rich soils by tracks and in leaf-litter

- **DISTRIBUTION**
Widespread; very common

DEATH CAP *Amanita phalloides*

The death cap is the most poisonous of all fungi to be found in the British Isles. Its ghostly all-white relative, the destroying angel, is also very poisonous but much rarer. The death cap's white gills (not brown or pinkish) and the volva at the base of the stem help distinguish it from most edible mushrooms.

If a fungus even remotely resembles the death cap, the golden rule is to look and admire but do not touch.

- **SIZE**
Cap 5–12cm (2–4¾in) wide; stem 8–15cm (3–6in) high

- **KEY FEATURES**
Olive-green cap, white gills, ragged ring on stem and baggy white volva (membranous sac) at base, half-buried in soil. As the name indicates, this fungus is deadly if ingested – do not even touch

- **SEASON**
Fruits from late summer through the autumn

- **HABITAT**
Woodland banks, usually on rich clay and under oak or beech trees

- **DISTRIBUTION**
Generally scarce, but in some years, can be common in favoured localities

WOOD MUSHROOM *Agaricus silvicola*

This medium to large fungus often grows in scattered 'troops', sometimes in pine woods, half buried in fallen needles. Its cap and stalk stain ochre-yellow if bruised. A mildly poisonous relative – the yellow-staining mushroom – can be identified by its flat top, smell of ink and the bright yellow base of its cut stem.

The large ring around the upper stem often becomes frayed as the fungus matures.

- **SIZE**
Cap 6–12cm (2½–4¾in) wide; stem 8–14cm (3–5½in) high

- **KEY FEATURES**
Cap and stalk cream, yellowing with age; skin and stem ring silky; gills pink, turning chocolate brown when spores mature. Fungus is distinguished by aniseed or almond-like smell and slender stem

- **SEASON**
Fruits from late summer through the autumn

- **HABITAT**
Generally woodland, rich soils, leaf litter and debris

- **DISTRIBUTION**
Generally scarce; may occur in mixed woodland or under pine trees on chalky soil

CHARCOAL BURNER *Russula cyanoxantha*

One of many basidiomycetes in the russula order, this large fungus occurs singly or in scattered groups. It grows under broad-leaved trees and in some years fruits in great numbers. Its oily or greasy gills are unlike those of most other russulas, which are dry and brittle.

The cap varies from bluish grey or purple to wine red, olive, green or brown, often as blotches on a single specimen.

● SIZE
Cap 5–12cm (2–4½in) wide; stem 5–10cm (2–4in) high

● KEY FEATURES
Characteristic crumbly texture, like bread sticks; gills oily or greasy; stem white and chunky; cap often multi-coloured; easily recognised

● SEASON
Fruits from summer to late autumn, peaking from August to early September

● HABITAT
Under woodland trees, especially beech, on poor soil; on top of banks rather than slopes

● DISTRIBUTION
Common in many localities

SAFFRON MILKCAP *Lactarius deliciosus*

The milkcaps differ from the russulas, with which they are grouped, because their flesh exudes a milky yellow substance when broken. The saffron milkcap grows either on its own or in scattered groups under pine trees – closely related fungi tend to grow under other tree species.

The cap of this fungus has a hollow centre and may develop a faint greenish tinge with age or bruising.

● SIZE
Cap 5–10cm (2–4in) wide; stem 3–7cm (1¼–2¾in) high

● KEY FEATURES
Funnel-shaped, orange-brown cap with faint concentric salmon-pink blotches; short stem pitted with orange; when damaged or broken, leaks saffron-yellow latex-like juice that turns carrot coloured and becomes acrid

● SEASON
Fruits in early autumn to October

● HABITAT
Under pines and spruce, generally on sandy soil

● DISTRIBUTION
Infrequent in many parts of Britain; most common in Scotland

CEP OR PENNY BUN *Boletus edulis*

The cep is classified with the boletes, a group of fungi with no gills. Highly valued in Europe for the table, it is known in Italian as *porcini*, in French as *cèpe* and in German as *steinpilz*. Associated with many different trees, it is often found growing among leaf litter or moss.

The thick, fleshy cap has a 'toasted' appearance on the outer surface, like a large bun. It is spongy to the touch.

● SIZE
Cap 6–20cm (2½–8in) or more wide; stem 7–18cm (2¾–7in) high

● KEY FEATURES
Cap often very large and has yellowish, spongy pores but no gills; pores are white, turning yellowish to olive with age; extremely stout stem has white net pattern of veins near top

● SEASON
Fruits through the autumn, most common in warm years

● HABITAT
Under a range of woodland trees, including beech, pine and birch, especially in Scotland, usually on well-drained, acid soils

● DISTRIBUTION
Very common in suitable sites

STINKHORN *Phallus impudicus*

The pungent odour emanating from the slimy spore-containing coating of the stinkhorn's cap can carry for long distances, but it is still often difficult to locate this fungus. The rapidly growing stem remains firmly rooted in a cup-shaped volva, or basal sac, formed by the egg-shaped structure from which it grows.

The thimble-shaped cap of the aptly named stinkhorn is instantly recognisable.

● SIZE
12–25cm (4¾–10in) tall; 'egg' about size of golf ball

● KEY FEATURES
Grows from whitish egg-shaped ball with firm, jelly-like consistency and white cords at base; mature fungus has spongy phallic shape; cap is covered with olive-green slime; smells of blocked drains or calor gas

● SEASON
Fruits from summer to autumn, peaking in September

● HABITAT
Woodland and parkland, especially around tree stumps, fallen branches and other dead rotting wood, often buried, among broad-leaved and coniferous trees

● DISTRIBUTION
Generally common

Three-pinnate ferns

Primitive, flowerless plants that thrive in damp, shady places, these ferns fill the autumnal air of woods with their sweet scent as they change colour and decay.

Very few plants have a genuinely worldwide distribution but bracken is one of them. It is without doubt one of the most successful colonising plants in the world today. Despite its ubiquitous nature, bracken is one of a select few British ferns that are three pinnate, that is its fronds are divided and sub-divided three times.

To establish how many times a fern is sub-divided, examine the whole plant, beginning at ground level. Follow the central stem – or 'rachis' – until you come to a secondary branch with toothed leaflets, or pinnae, on each side. The majority of British ferns do not branch any more than this, but the three-pinnate ferns have a third division, which carries the rows of individual leaflets, now called pinnules.

Creeping rhizomes

As with other ferns, bracken produces millions of spores each season. Unlike most other ferns, however, it is not dependent upon them for propagation. Instead, it can spread rapidly across huge areas via underground rootlike horizontal stems – known as rhizomes – that grow from the parent plant.

Less than 100 years ago, bracken was harvested by commoners who used the fronds for animal bedding instead of straw. This restricted

DANGER!

Bracken is poisonous. Do not try to pick it and always wash your hands after handling it.

◀ Bracken adds colour to the woodland scene for much of the year, from the vivid green of young spring fronds to the glorious copper browns of autumn and winter.

the fern's growth and prevented it from becoming invasive. Bracken is rarely harvested these days and now grows largely unchecked, often stifling other plants. If it is not controlled, its vigour can pose a serious threat to the number of plants and animals that can thrive in some woods and on certain heaths.

Emerging 'bishop's staffs' or 'shepherd's crooks' in late spring are the first signs of bracken growth. Bishop's staffs – closely coiled immature fronds – occur in most ferns, but are especially obvious in bracken.

Broad buckler fern grows in dense tufts. Each one looks rather like a shuttlecock head.

Related ferns

In contrast to robust, aggressive bracken, one of the most delicate-looking British ferns, the parsley fern, is also three-pinnate. A close look at these ferns in midsummer will reveal two types of frond. Although quite similar, the outer fronds are sterile whereas the middle fronds are fertile. They carry spores on the undersides, which are protected by inrolled leaf margins. In autumn, the fronds turn a bright rusty brown colour, which persists throughout winter.

A third member of the three-pinnate family is the tall broad buckler fern, which thrives on fertile, acid soils in shady wooded areas.

▼ Parsley fern fronds poke out between rocks in mountain scree. This fern prefers a hostile environment such as this, which other ferns would not tolerate.

LETHAL COCKTAIL

While animals can often evade potential predators, plants cannot. This does not mean that all plants provide ready meals for the next hungry animal that passes by. Many plants protect themselves with an array of chemicals that they have developed over millions of years to help ward off, maim or even kill plant-eating animals.

Bracken is one such plant. Its tissues are loaded with a cocktail of some of the nastiest chemicals known, and are capable of discouraging even the most persistent herbivore. The deadliest substance in bracken is the respiratory poison hydrogen cyanide. The plant is able to regulate the amount of this poison produced in its tissues over the growing season. The most concentrated amounts occur during its fastest growth stage, between May and July. At this time, its fresh leaves are soft and appealing, and damage to the plant could potentially be most harmful.

As the season progresses, the concentration of hydrogen cyanide begins to diminish, but woe betide any insect that still attempts to feed on bracken. Another substance within its tissues mimics the insect moulting hormone ecdysone. This induces insects that eat bracken to shed their exoskeleton prematurely, leading to abnormal growth and development and often proving fatal. After eating bracken, one insect was recorded growing three layers of chitin – the outer covering of an insect's body – over its head. As a result, the insect was unable to feed and eventually starved to death.

Despite these potentially damaging toxic substances, the young uncurled fronds of bracken are often cooked and eaten by people in South-east Asia, even though the plant may be carcinogenic to humans if eaten in sufficient quantity.

▼ For butterflies such as this dark green fritillary, stands of bracken may provide convenient sunny perches, but little more. Very few insects feed directly on bracken.

▲ The outline of bracken fronds is triangular and the stems of mature plants are hard and rigid. Bracken fills copses and covers heaths and moors with its luxuriant growth.

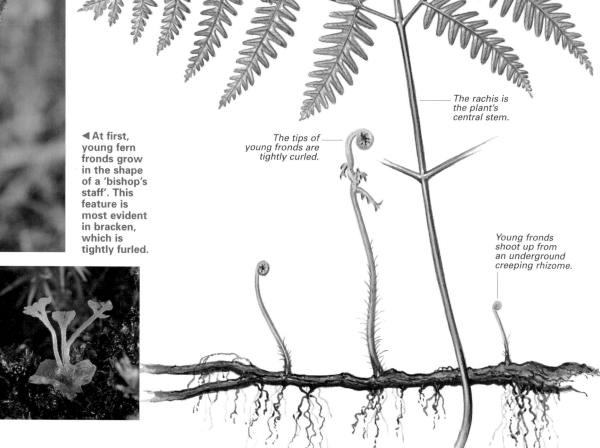

Bracken or brake
Pteridium aquilinum

Almost all fronds of bracken are fertile. The spores are hidden on the underside of the pinnules.

The rachis is the plant's central stem.

The tips of young fronds are tightly curled.

Young fronds shoot up from an underground creeping rhizome.

◄ At first, young fern fronds grow in the shape of a 'bishop's staff'. This feature is most evident in bracken, which is tightly furled.

► Like other ferns, bracken can reproduce sexually via spores. These grow into a green scale-like disc called the prothallus from which a tiny young fern develops.

THREE-PINNATE FERN FACT FILE

● **Parsley fern**
Cryptogramma crispa

Habitat and distribution
Often inhabits hostile environments. Occurs on acid soils, on walls, rocks and scree slopes in hilly and mountainous regions of western Britain; most common in North Wales, the Lake District and northern Ireland.

Size 15–30cm (6–12in)

Key features
Bright green tufts of non-fertile lobed, toothed pinnae give parsley-like appearance; erect, fertile fronds with unlobed, untoothed pinnae grow in centre; foliage dies back in winter from December–mid-April

Spores
Located under inrolled margins of leaflets, or pinnules, on the fertile fronds; ripen July–August

Parsley fern
Cryptogramma crispa

Vegetative or non-fertile lobed, toothed fronds have densely tufted, bright green pinnules.

Fertile fronds with narrower sets of unlobed, untoothed pinnules grow erect from centre of clump.

The stalks have scales at the base only.

Young fronds are pale green and curled at tips.

The creeping rootstock sends out fine tendrils to gain purchase through the soil.

▲ Parsley fern has bright green, vegetative fronds with curly dissected leaflets. Its resemblance to parsley is purely visual – this plant must not be substituted for the kitchen herb.

▲ Cracks and crevices in dry-stone walls provide ideal rootholds for parsley fern. Such features are common in upland areas.

Broad buckler fern
Dryopteris dilatata

THREE-PINNATE FERN
FACT FILE

● **Broad buckler fern**
Dryopteris dilatata
Habitat and distribution
Common in woodland and
other shady places throughout
Britain and Ireland; prefers
fairly acid soils and likes
drier habitats than many
native ferns
Size Up to 1.5m (5ft)

Key features
Olive green, triangular fronds,
arranged into a densely tufted
plant; stem has dark streak
down centre; fronds appear
April–November
Spores
Spores on underside of fronds
protected by kidney-shaped
scales; spores ripen
July–August

*The fronds are
triangular and
spreading.*

*The pinnules are
dark green and
have serrated
edges.*

*Spores are
borne on the
underside of
the pinnules.*

▼ **The leaves of the broad
buckler fern form large
spreading clumps from
April to November.**

◄ **On the undersides of
the pinnules, spores are
borne in minute sacs
known as sporangia. The
spores are dispersed by
the wind or when the
frond is brushed by a
passing animal or rambler.**

Spurges and mercuries

The bright yellow-green flowers of many spurges and mercuries continue to flourish as summer turns to autumn. They spread across open deciduous woodland, fields and gardens, their stems oozing milky sap when cut or torn.

Spurges and mercuries are Britain's native representatives of the family Euphorbiaceae. All the plants in this large family have a milky, acrid latex juice – tropical examples include the rubber tree and the castor oil plant. Fleshy desert spurges are Old World counterparts of American cacti.

Twelve native and 10 introduced spurges are found in the British Isles – another, the hairy spurge, became extinct in 1941. These plants are annuals, biennials or perennials with erect stems. The leaves are narrow, oval or wedge-shaped, often stalkless, unlobed and untoothed. They cover the stems densely and may overlap. In the caper spurge and purple spurge the leaves are in opposite pairs.

The tiny flowers are green or yellowish and arranged in a structure called the cyathium. This is unique to spurges and comprises a cluster of male flowers, each reduced to a single pollen-bearing stamen. These surround a stalked female flower with a triple-lobed ovary from which project three often-forked styles connecting it to the stigmas. These receive the pollen. After fertilisation, the ovary develops into a capsule, which releases three seeds when ripe.

Flower clusters are surrounded by tiny, scale-like modified leaves called bracts, and have pairs of glistening nectar glands. Opposite pairs of larger, pale green or yellowish green petal-like bracts surround the whole floral structure.

Woodland habitat

Most mercuries occur in woodland. They have small green flowers, oval leaves in opposite pairs and, like spurges, produce milky sap. Male flowers grouped in erect, tassel-like clusters have nine to 12 stamens. Smaller clusters of female flowers have double-lobed ovaries, each of which produces two seeds.

Dog's mercury is found in broad-leaved woodland. New shoots bearing wind-pollinated flowers emerge in early spring before the trees produce any leaves, which would impede the movement of pollen.

Wood spurge thrives in open or coppiced woodland and old hedgerows. It forms conspicuous yellow-flowered clumps and can be abundant. Rarer spurges include upright spurge, which prefers coppices on limestone soils in the Welsh Marches, and Irish spurge, found in south-west Ireland, parts of Cornwall and one site in north Devon.

Open ground

Many of the spurges and annual mercury are plants of cultivated or disturbed ground – land that has been dug over at one time. The most common of these in the south is petty spurge, which can grow in huge numbers in flower beds and ornamental tubs. Sun spurge, a yellower, more robust plant, often grows on farmland and caper spurge is a striking plant of cottage gardens. Most wild caper spurges are escapes from cultivated varieties.

There are three coastal spurges. Sea spurge is found on beaches from the Lake District round to north Norfolk and on the north, east and south-west coasts of Ireland. Portland spurge grows on beaches, too, and on the grass and heath of clifftops. It thrives on the Welsh coast. The third coastal species, the prostrate purple spurge, has not been recorded in the British Isles since 1976.

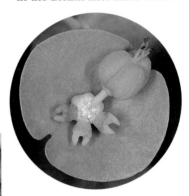

▲ The tiny, bright yellowish green flowers of wood spurge are held in saucer-like bracts. The swollen fruits contain three seeds and burst when ripe.

◄ Common throughout England and Wales, petty spurge is abundant in gardens, arable crops and disturbed ground. Its tiny yellowish flowers appear from April to November or even later in mild weather.

DANGER!

The white sap or latex in the stems and leaves of spurges can irritate the skin and is poisonous if eaten. The mercuries are also poisonous.

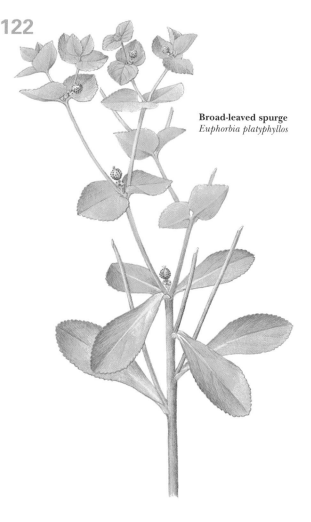

Broad-leaved spurge
Euphorbia platyphyllos

SPURGE FACT FILE

● **Broad-leaved spurge**
Euphorbia platyphyllos
Habitat and distribution
Scarce on waste or cultivated land on heavier soils in southern England
Size 30–80cm (12–32in) tall
Key features
A hairless or downy annual with numerous, erect reddish stems; leaves narrowly elliptical or heart-shaped, outer half finely saw-toothed; fruits hairless with rounded warts
Flowering time
June–September

● **Upright spurge**
Euphorbia serrulata
Habitat and distribution
Rare; found in woodland clearings and coppices on limestone in Gloucestershire and Gwent
Size 20–80cm (8–32in) tall
Key features
Similar to broad-leaved spurge but more slender and hairless; leaves narrower; fruits with tall cylindrical warts
Flowering time
June–September

● **Sun spurge**
Euphorbia helioscopia
Habitat and distribution
Common on cultivated land in England, Wales and Ireland, especially on lime-rich soils; scarcer and more coastal in Scotland
Size 10–50cm (4–20in) tall
Key features
A hairless, yellowish green annual with rather stout stems sometimes branched above; leaves oval or wedge-shaped, blunt, tapering to base, finely saw-toothed; flowers bright yellowish at first; fruits smooth
Flowering time
April–November, often continuing throughout mild winters

● **Hairy or downy spurge**
Euphorbia villosa
A hairy perennial that was once a common plant of coppices. It was first recorded in a woodland near Bath in the 16th century, where it persisted until about 1937. The general cessation of coppicing in around 1900 was responsible for its final extinction in the British Isles

Sun spurge is the only common spurge of the British Isles with toothed leaves. Its golden green foliage brightens waste and cultivated ground throughout the lowlands.

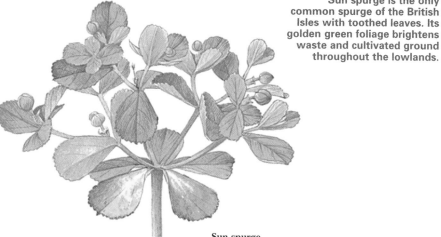

Upright spurge
Euphorbia serrulata

Sun spurge
Euphorbia helioscopia

SPURGE FACT FILE

● **Petty spurge**
Euphorbia peplus
Habitat and distribution
Common on cultivated land throughout Britain and Ireland; scarcer in Scotland
Size 10–30cm (4–12in) tall
Key features
A hairless, rather pale green annual with erect, branched, often reddish stems; leaves triangular-oval, stalked, untoothed; flower-heads green, bracts around flower clusters triangular-oval; fruits hairless with shallow wavy keels
Flowering time
April–November (and throughout mild winters)

● **Dwarf spurge**
Euphorbia exigua
Habitat and distribution
Widespread but local on cultivated ground, especially on lime-rich soils and in central and south-eastern England
Size 10–20cm (4–8in) tall
Key features
Similar to petty spurge, but smaller and slenderer; leaves greyish, narrow, oblong, stalkless; bracts around flower clusters spear-shaped; fruits smooth, not keeled
Flowering time
June–September

● **Portland spurge**
Euphorbia portlandica
Habitat and distribution
Sand dunes, low cliffs and banks on coasts of Britain, north to Galloway on the west side and to Hampshire on the east; in Ireland mainly on east coast but also on south-west and north coasts
Size 10–40cm (4–16in) tall
Key features
Erect, often red-tinged hairless biennial or short-lived perennial; leaves narrowly oval or spear-shaped, untoothed, slightly fleshy, with minute points; fruits slightly rough, hairless
Flowering time
April–September

● **Sea spurge**
Euphorbia paralias
Habitat and distribution
Sand or shingle beaches on coasts north to Solway Firth in west, the Wash in east; in Ireland mainly on east coast but also on south-west and north coasts
Size 20–60cm (8–24in) tall
Key features
Similar to Portland spurge, but with tougher rootstock; leaves pale greyish green, fleshy, oblong, midrib obscure below; fruits wrinkled
Flowering time
July–October

● **Leafy spurge**
Euphorbia esula
Habitat and distribution
A European plant naturalised on waste ground, mainly in southern and eastern England
Size 40–100cm (16–40in) tall
Key features
Perennial with creeping rhizomes and numerous erect stems, patch-forming; leaves club-shaped, untoothed; fruits rough, hairless
Flowering time
June–August

● **Cypress spurge**
Euphorbia cyparissias
Habitat and distribution
A garden plant naturalised on waste ground except in Ireland, most of Wales and Scotland; perhaps native, but rare, on chalk grassland in south-eastern England, abundant at one site in Wiltshire
Size 20–40cm (8–16in) tall
Key features
Similar to leafy spurge but smaller and much less robust; leaves densely crowded, about 2mm (1/8in) wide, narrowly oblong
Flowering time
April–July

● **Caper spurge**
Euphorbia lathyris
Habitat and distribution
Widespread in gardens in England and Wales; scarce elsewhere; occasionally in woodland, native in south
Size 50–200cm (20in–80in) tall
Key features
A tall hairless biennial with robust, erect stems, branched above; leaves greyish green, narrowly oblong to broadly spear-shaped, toothless, in opposite pairs; fruits large, three-sided, smooth, hairless, resembling capers but poisonous
Flowering time
June–August

● **Wood spurge**
Euphorbia amygdaloides
Habitat and distribution
Common in woodland and shady hedge banks in Wales and southern England; also near Bandon, County Cork, Ireland
Size 40–90cm (16–36in) tall
Key features
Clump-forming, downy perennial with erect, unbranched stems; leaves dark green, oblong or elliptical, untoothed, 5–10cm (2–4in) long; bracts around flower clusters in fused pairs; fruits slightly rough
Flowering time
March–May

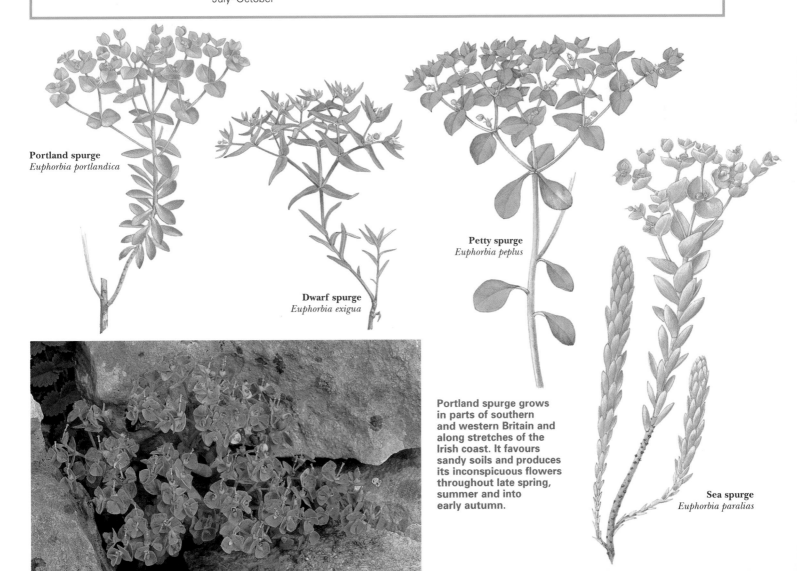

Portland spurge
Euphorbia portlandica

Dwarf spurge
Euphorbia exigua

Petty spurge
Euphorbia peplus

Portland spurge grows in parts of southern and western Britain and along stretches of the Irish coast. It favours sandy soils and produces its inconspicuous flowers throughout late spring, summer and into early autumn.

Sea spurge
Euphorbia paralias

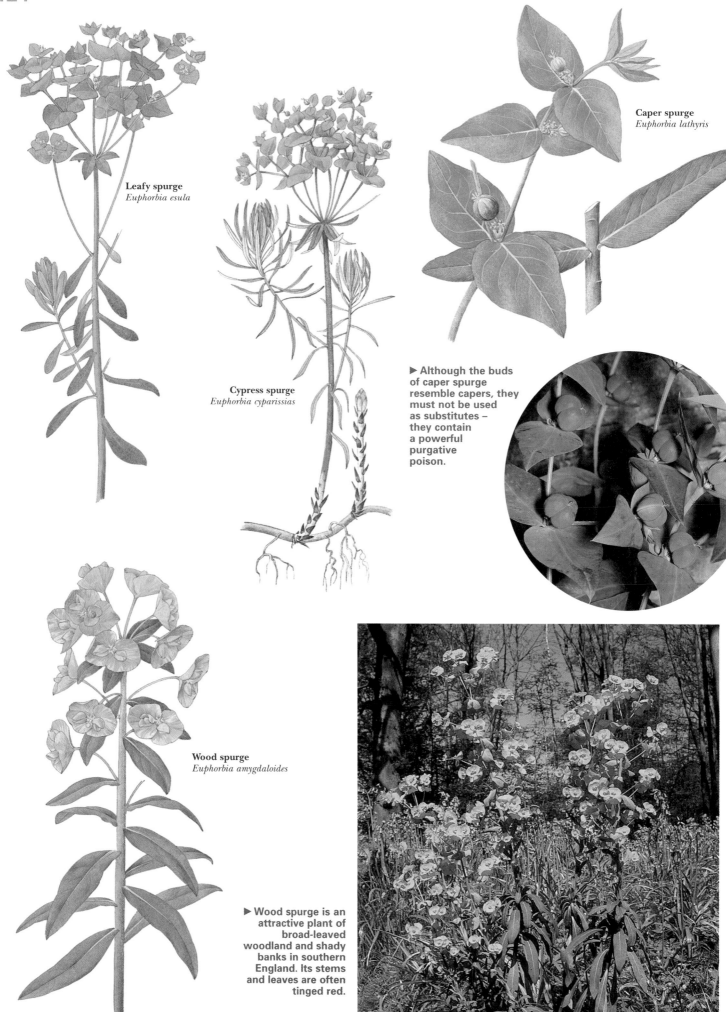

Leafy spurge
Euphorbia esula

Cypress spurge
Euphorbia cyparissias

Caper spurge
Euphorbia lathyris

► Although the buds
of caper spurge
resemble capers, they
must not be used
as substitutes –
they contain
a powerful
purgative
poison.

Wood spurge
Euphorbia amygdaloides

► Wood spurge is an
attractive plant of
broad-leaved
woodland and shady
banks in southern
England. Its stems
and leaves are often
tinged red.

SPURGE AND MERCURY FACT FILE

● **Purple spurge**
Euphorbia peplis
Habitat and distribution
Last reliably recorded on Alderney, Channel Islands in 1976
Size Stems 5–10cm (2–4in) long
Key features
A prostrate annual with purplish red branched stems; leaves deep green, curled, oval, untoothed, in opposite pairs; flower clusters solitary in stem forks and leaf angles; fruits smooth
Flowering time
July–September

● **Irish spurge**
Euphorbia hyberna
Habitat and distribution
Woodlands, scrub, hedgerows and rough grassland in south-western Ireland; rare in County Donegal and south-western England
Size 30–60cm (12–24in) tall
Key features
A slightly downy, clump-forming perennial with erect, little-branched stems; leaves 5–8cm (2–3in) long, oblong to spear-shaped, untoothed; bracts around flower clusters, bright yellowish, showy, heart-shaped; fruits with prominent cylindrical warts
Flowering time
April–July

● **Sweet spurge**
Euphorbia dulcis
Habitat and distribution
A European plant occasionally naturalised in shady places
Size 20–50cm (8–20in) tall
Key features
Similar to Irish spurge but leaves 3–5cm (1¼–2in) wide, untoothed or finely saw-toothed; bracts around flower clusters green at first, soon becoming dark purple, cut off abruptly at base
Flowering time
May–July

● **Dog's mercury**
Mercurialis perennis
Habitat and distribution
Woodland, shady hedge banks, crevices of limestone pavements and mountains over most of Britain; rare in Ireland
Size 20–40cm (8–16in) tall
Key features
A downy perennial, forming extensive patches, with numerous erect, unbranched stems; leaves dark green, oval or elliptical, toothed, 4–8cm (1½–3in) long; male and female flowers on separate plants; male flower clusters 5–12cm (2–4¾in) long, erect, tassel-like; female clusters stalked
Flowering time
February–April

● **Annual mercury**
Mercurialis annua
Habitat and distribution
Widespread but local on cultivated and disturbed ground, mainly in southern and eastern Britain; in Ireland only around Dublin and on south coast
Size 10–50cm (4–20in) tall
Key features
Similar to dog's mercury but a hairless, branched annual; leaves pale green; female flower clusters almost stalkless
Flowering time
April–October

Purple spurge
Euphorbia peplis

Sweet spurge
Euphorbia dulcis

Irish spurge
Euphorbia hyberna

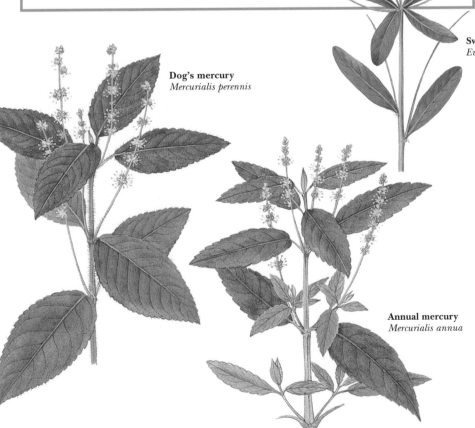

Dog's mercury
Mercurialis perennis

Annual mercury
Mercurialis annua

WILDLIFE WATCH

Where do spurges and mercuries grow?

● Many spurges and dog's mercury grow in woodland, especially in clearings or where trees have been coppiced. Wood spurge is widespread in southern England.

● Irish spurge is common in south-western Ireland.

● Petty spurge and sun spurge, along with the less common dwarf spurge and annual mercury, can be found growing on cultivated ground. Sometimes caper spurge and cypress spurge invade untended gardens.

● Look out for Portland spurge and sea spurge on western coasts in particular, often where sand dunes merge into beach.

Index

Page numbers in *italic* refer to illustrations

A

adelgids (*Adelgis abietis*) 26
agarics 79, 112
  fly (*Amanita muscari*) 8, *111*, 112, 114, *114*
  verdigris (*Stropharia aeruginosa*) 81, *81*
agrimony (*Agrimonia eupatoria*) 70, 72, *73*
  bastard (*Aremonia agrimonioides*) 72, *73*
  fragrant (*Agrimonia procera*) 72, *73*
anemone, wood 26
ants 67
  yellow (*Lasius flavus*) *106*
aphids 14, 108, 109
artichoke gall 108, *109*
ascomycetes 79, 112
ash tree 8
aspen *109*
avens 70
  mountain (*Dryas octopetala*) 70, 72, *73*
  water (*Geum rivale*) 72, *72*
  wood (*Geum urbanum*) 72, *72*

B

badger 18, 29, 30, *31*
basidiomycetes 79, 112
bats 19, 23, 88–92, *88–92*
  barbastelle (*Barbastella barbastellus*) *89*, 91, *91*
  Bechstein's (*Myotis bechsteini*) 88, *89*, 92, *92*
  brown long-eared (*Plecotus auritus*) *89*, *89*, 91, *91*
  Daubenton's (*Myotis daubentonii*) *89*, *89*, 92, *92*
  greater horseshoe (*Rhinolophus ferrumequinum*) *89*, *89*, 90, *90*
  Leisler's (*Nyctalus leisleri*) *89*, *89*, 90, *90*
  lesser horseshoe (*Rhinolophus hipposideros*) *89*, *89*, 90, *90*
  long-eared 29, *29*
  mouse-eared 88
  Natterer's (*Myotis nattereri*) *89*, 92, *92*
  noctule (*Nyctalus noctula*) 29, 89, *89*, 90, *90*
  pipistrelle (*Pipistrellus pipistrellus*) 29, 88, *89*, 91, *91*
  serotine (*Eptesicus serotinus*) *89*, 91, *91*
  vesper 89
  whiskered (*Myotis mystacinus*) *89*, 92, *92*
bean gall 107
bedeguar gall 107
beech (*Fagus sylvatica*) 8, 20–23, *20–23*, 32, *34*
beechwood sickener (*Russula nobilis*) 23, *23*
berries 70–74, *70–74*
bilberry 26
birds
  in brambles 14
  flocks 7, 9
  in larch forests 27
  in New Forest 36
  see also individual types of bird
bittersweet (*Solanum dulcamara*) 7, 75, 76, *76*

blackberry (*Rubus fruticosus*) 7, 12–15, *12–15*, 70, *70*, 71, *71*
blackbird 28, 61
blackcap 101
blackthorn 7, *7*, 110
blewit (*Lepista personata*) 80, *80*
  wood (*Lepista nuda*) 113, *113*
bluebell 26
blue butterflies
  common 7
  silver-studded 36
bluelegs (*Lepista personata*) 80, *80*
blusher (*Amanita rubescens*) 114, *114*
boletes 112
  bay (*Boletus badius*) 26
  larch (*Suillus grevillei*) 26
  Suillus viscidus 26
bracken (*Pteridium aquilinum*) 116–17, 118, *118*
brambles (*Rubus fruticosus*) 7, 12–15, *12–15*, 26, 70, *70*, 71, *71*
brambling *22*, *33*
bridewort (*Spiraea* x *pseudosalicifolia*) 70, 74, *74*
buff arches' moth 14
bullfinch 61
buntings 7
  reed 61
butterflies
  on brambles 14
  caterpillars 67
  grassland in autumn 7–8
  in New Forest 36

C

caddis flies 67, *67*
caterpillars *9*, 14, 66–67, *66*
celandine, lesser 26
ceps (*Boletus edulis*) 112, 115, *115*
chaffinch 7, 21
chalk downs, ridgeways 16
chanterelle (*Cantharellus cibarius*) 112, 113, *113*
charcoal burner (*Russula cyanoxantha*) 115, *115*
cherry gall 108
cicada, New Forest 35–36
clary, meadow 19
clematis *6*
cloudberry (*Rubus chamaemorus*) 13, 70, *70*, 71, *71*
clouded yellow butterfly 7–8
clover 7
cock's-eggs (*Salpichroa originalifolia*) 77, *77*
cock's-foot grass 40, 43
cocoons, caterpillars 66–67, *66*
comma butterfly 14
conifer plantations 24, 33
copper butterfly, small 7, *18*, 19
coppiced trees 8–9, 85, *85*
craneflies 19
crane's-bill, meadow 19
crickets
  bush *13*, 14
  wood 22
crossbill, common *26*, 27
crows *45*, 60
currant gall 108

D

damselflies 36
  blue 36
dance fly (*Hilara maura*) 67
darters, black 36

death cap (*Amanita phalloides*) 8, 23, 114, *114*
deer 13, 15, 17, 18, 32, 33
  fallow 35
  muntjac 30
  red *7*, 35, *36*
  roe *13*, *28*, 30, 35
  sika 30, 35
dewberry (*Rubus caesius*) 13, *13*, 71, *71*
docks 19
dogwood 110
dormouse 9, 12, *12*, 21, 23, *29*, 30, 84–87, *84–87*
doves
  stock 23
  turtle 100
dragonflies 19, 36
dropwort (*Filipendula vulgaris*) 70, 74, *74*
Duke of Argyll's teaplant (*Lycium barbarum*) 77, *77*
dunnock 14, 15, *15*

E

earthballs 112
earth-fan (*Thelephora terrestris*) 27
earth-stars 112
  barometer 78
earth tongues 78, 79
earthworms 31, *48*
eggar moth *66*
elm 109
emperor moth 36

F

fairy-ring champignon (*Marasmius oreades*) 78, *78*, 81, *81*
ferns 18
  broad buckler (*Dryopteris dilatata*) 117, *117*, 120, *120*
  hart's-tongue 18, *18*, 22, *23*
  parsley (*Cryptogramma crispa*) 117, *117*, 119, *119*
  three-pinnate 116–20, *116–20*
field mushroom (*Agaricus campestris*) 8, 81, *81*
finches 7, 17
firecrest (*Regulus ignicapillus*) 97, *97*, 98
fleas 67
flies 67
  picture-winged (*Tephritidae*) 110
  Urophora cardui 110, *110*
flycatchers 8
forests, larch 24–27, *24–27*
  see also woodland
fox 18, 30, *30*, 35
fritillaries
  dark green *117*
  silver-washed 36
frogs 31
fruit, berries 12–15, *12–15*, 42, 70–74, *70–74*
fungi
  bird's nest 112
  blood foot *36*
  bracket 111, 112
  grassland species 8, 78–82, *78–82*
  honey (*Armillaria mellea*) 8, 113, *113*
  jelly 112
  in larch forests 26–27
  in New Forest 35
  plums-and-custard (*Tricholomopsis rutilans*) 26–27

porcelain (*Oudemansiella mucida*) 23
woodland species 8, 111–15, *111–15*
yellow antler (*Calocera viscosa*) *26*, 27

G

gall aphids 109
  Adelges 109
  Cryptomyzus ribis 109
  Eriosoma ulmi 109
  Pemphigus bursarius 109
  Pemphigus spyrothecae 109
  Tetraneura ulmi 109
gall flies, *Phytomyza ilicis 108*
gall midges 107–8, 109–10
  Craneiobia corni 110
  Dasineura crataegi 110
  Dasineura violae 110
  Harmandia globuli 109
  Jaapiella veronicae 110
  Rondaniola bursaria 110
  Taxomyia taxi 109
galls 107–10, *107–10*
gall sawflies, *Pontania proxima* 110
gall wasps 14, 107, 108, *108*
  Andricus kollari 108
  Andricus quercuscalicis 109
  Biorhiza pallida 109
  Diplolepis rosae 107, 109
  Neuroterus numismalis 108, *110*
  Neuroterus quercusbaccarum 108
garlic, hedge 19
gatekeeper butterfly 14, 26
gentian, fringed *9*
goldcrest (*Regulus regulus*) 9, 27, 93–98, *93–98*
goldfinch 6, 7, 19, *19*, *24*
grasshopper *65*
grassland fungi 78–82, *78–82*
grayling butterfly 36
greenfinch 7
green lanes 16–19, *18*, *19*
ground ivy 110

H

hammock webs, spiders 66
hare, brown 18, *18*
harvestmen 68–69, *68–69*
  Homalenotus quadridentatus 69
  Leiobunum rotundum 68, 69
  Megabunus diadema 69
  Mitopus morio 69
  Nemastoma bimaculatum 69
  Odiellus spinosus 69
  Oligolophus tridens 69
  Opilio parietinus 69
  Paroligolophus agrestis 69
  Phalangium opilio 69, *69*
  Trogulus tricarinatus 68
hawfinch 35
hawk-moths
  eyed 31
  poplar 31
hawthorn 7, *17*, 110
hazel, common (*Corylus avellana*) 8, 85, *85*
hearing, nocturnal animals 30
hedgehog 29, 63
henbane (*Hyoscyamus niger*) 75, *75*, 77, *77*
herb bennet (*Geum urbanum*) 72, 72
hobby *33*, 36
hogweed 19, *19*
hollow ways 18, *18*
holly *15*, 32, 35

honeysuckle *15, 16*, 30–31
hornbeam 35
horn of plenty (*Craterellus cornucopioides*) 113, *113*
horse fly 26
horse mushroom (*Agaricus arvensis*) 78, 81, *81*
hoverflies 14, 19, 26

I
inkcaps 79, 111
    shaggy (*Coprinus comatus*) 8, 82, *82*

J
jackdaw 23, 60
jay 9, 28, 35, 62
judge's wig (*Coprinus comatus*) 82, *82*

K
kestrel 18
knapweeds 19, 110
knopper gall 109, *109*

L
lacewings 67
ladybirds 14
    larch (*Aphidecta obliterata*) 26, *26*
lanes, green 16–19, *18, 19*
larches
    European (*Larix decidua*) 24–27, *24–27*
    Japanese (*Larix kaempferi*) 25, 27
    Larix x *eurolepis* 25
leaf miner, moth caterpillar
    bramble 14
    holly *108*
lighthouse gall 110, *110*
lime tree 110
ling 26
linnet 7, 61, 100
linyphiid spiders 66, *66*
liverworts 18
lizard, sand 35, *35*
lobster moth 22

M
magpie (*Pica pica*) 58–63, *58–63*
maple 110
marble gall 108, *108*
martin, house 18–19
meadowsweet (*Filipendula ulmaria*) 70, 74, *74*
mercuries 121
    annual (*Mercurialis annua*) 121, 125, *125*
    dog's (*Mercurialis perennis*) 26, 121, 125, *125*
mice
    harvest (*Micromys minutus*) 18, *18*, 40–45, *40–45*
    wood *13*, 17, 18, 29, *30*
midges 19, 109–10
milkcaps
    rufous (*Lactarius rufus*) 24, 26
    saffron (*Lactarius deliciosus*) 115, *115*
millipedes *31*
mite galls 110, *110*
money spiders 66
moneywort, Cornish 18
morels 79, 112
mosses 18
    white fork 22
moths
    caterpillars *9*, 14
    nocturnal 30–31
mule pheasants 104
mushrooms *see* fungi
mycelium, fungi 79

N
nail gall 110
New Forest 32–37, *32–37*
nightjar 36

nightshades 75–77
    annual 75
    black (*Solanum nigrum*) 76, *76*
    deadly (*Atropa belladonna*) 75, *75*, 76, *76*
    hairy (*Solanum villosum*) 76, *76*
    leafy-fruited (*Solanum sarachoides*) 76, *76*
    small (*Solanum triflorum*) 76, *76*
    woody (*Solanum dulcamara*) 76, *76*
night vision 29–30
nocturnal animals 28–31, *28–31*
nuthatch *8*, 21, *22*, 23, 35

O
oak *8*, 32, 33, 35
    Turkey 109
oak apples 107, 108, 109
orb web spiders *64–65*, 65–66
    four-spotted (*Araneus quadratus*) 65
orchids
    bird's-nest 22
    ghost 22, *22*
    heath-spotted *37*
owls 23
    barn *9, 16*, 18, 44, 57
    little (*Athene noctua*) 30, 52–57, *52–57*
    long-eared 27
    tawny 28–29, *29*, 57

P
pale tussock moth, larva *9*
parasol mushrooms (*Macrolepiota procera*) 8, 78, *78*, 79, 82, *82*
penny bun (*Boletus edulis*) 115, *115*
pheasant (*Phasianus colchicus*) 28, 99–104, *99–104*
    black 103
    crested argus 99
    golden 99, 103, *103*
    green 103
    Lady Amherst's 99, 103, *103*
    Reeve's 103
pigeon, wood 28
pineapple gall 109
pine marten 30
pinkgills 78
pirri-pirri-bur (*Acaena novaezelandiae*) 70, 74, *74*
planthoppers 66
poisons
    bracken 117
    fungi 8, 78, 80, 81, 111, 113, 114
    nightshades 75, 77
pony, New Forest *32–33*, 33, 35
poplar 109
primrose *18*
psyllids 108
puffballs 35, 79
    giant (*Calvatia gigantea*) 8, 78, 82, *82*

R
rabbit 15, 17, 18
ragwort 7, 19
raspberry (*Rubus idaeus*) 70, 71, *71*
red admiral butterfly 14
redcurrant 109
red spider mite 67
ringlet butterfly 67
robin 15, 61
robin's pincushion 107, *107*, 108, 109
rook 6, *6*
rose, wild 7
rose family 70–74
russulas 112

S
sawflies 67, 108, 110
scarlet hood (*Hygrocybe coccinea*) 80, *80*
scorpionfly 26, *26*

sea slater 106, *106*
service tree *8*
sheep 13, 33, *60*
shrews
    common 29, 49, 50
    pygmy (*Sorex minutus*) 46–51, *46–51*
silk
    caddis flies 67, *67*
    caterpillars 66–67, *66*
    spiders 64–66, *65*
silk moth (*Bombyx mori*) 67, *67*
skimmer, keeled 36
skipper butterfly 67
skylark 61
sloes 7, *7*
slugs 23
    ashy grey 23
    lemon 23
    leopard 31, *31*
snails 23
    cheese *22*, 23
    garden *49*
snake, smooth 35, *35*
soldier beetle 19
songbirds, magpie predation 61, 63
spangle galls 107, 108, *108*
    common 108
    silk button 108, *110*
sparrow, tree 61
sparrowhawk 9
speckled wood butterfly 26, *27*
speedwell, germander 110
spiders 68
    Amaurobius 66, *66*
    Dysdera crocata 106
    garden (*Araneus diadenatus*) 65
    house 64, *66*
    Theridion sisyphium 66
    webs 8, 64–66, *64–66*
spiraea, willow (*Spiraea* x *pseudosalicifolia*) 74, *74*
spores, fungi 78, 79, 111
spruce 109
spurges 121–25
    broad-leaved (*Euphorbia platyphyllos*) 122, *122*
    caper (*Euphorbia lathyris*) 121, 123, *124*
    cypress (*Euphorbia cyparissias*) 123, *124*
    downy (*Euphorbia villosa*) 122
    dwarf (*Euphorbia exigua*) 123, *123*
    hairy (*Euphorbia villosa*) 121, 122
    Irish (*Euphorbia hyberna*) 121, 125, *125*
    leafy (*Euphorbia esula*) 123, *124*
    petty (*Euphorbia peplus*) 121, *121*, 123, *123*
    Portland (*Euphorbia portlandica*) 121, 123, *123*
    purple (*Euphorbia peplis*) 121, 125, *125*
    sea (*Euphorbia paralis*) 121, 123, *123*
    sun (*Euphorbia helioscopia*) 121, 122, *122*
    sweet (*Euphorbia dulcis*) 125, *125*
    upright (*Euphorbia serrulata*) 121, 122, *122*
    wood (*Euphorbia amygdaloides*) 26, 121, *121*, 123, *124*
'sputnik' gall 108
squirrels 23
    grey *8*, 9, 21, 35
stag beetle 35, 36
stinkhorn (*Phallus impudicus*) *111*, 112, 115, *115*
stitchwort, greater 26
stone bramble (*Rubus saxatilis*) 13, *13*, 71, *71*
strawberry, wild (*Fragaria vesca*) 70, 72, *72, 73*
swallow 18–19, 36

swift 36
sycamore 110

T
tansy 7
teasel *19*
thistles 6, 19, 110
thorn-apple (*Datura stramonium*) 77, *77*
thrushes 9
    song 15, 61
tits 101
    blue 9
    coal 9, 27, *27*
    great 21
    long-tailed 9, 14–15, *15*
    marsh 9
toads 31, *31*
toadstools *see* fungi
tracks, ancient 16–19, *18, 19*
traveller's joy 7
treecreeper 35
trees, coppiced 8–9, 85, *85*
    see also forests, woodland *and individual types of tree*
truffles 112

V
violets 110
voles *9*, 17
    bank *7*, *17*, 18, 29

W
warblers 15
    Dartford 36, *36*
    garden 101
    Pallas's (*Phylloscopus proregulus*) 95–96
    willow 100
    yellow-browed (*Phylloscopus inornatus*) 95–96
wasps *6*
waxcaps 78, 79
    blackening (*Hygrocybe nigrescens*) 80, *80*
    conical (*Hygrocybe conica*) 80, *80*
    scarlet (*Hygrocybe coccinea*) 80, *80*
weasel 19, 44
webs
    caterpillars' 66–67, *66*
    spiders' 8, 64–66, *64–66*
weeping widow (*Lacrymaria lacrymabunda*) 82, *82*
weevils 19, 108
white admiral butterfly 36
whitethroat 14
willow 110
winter moth 31
witches' brooms *109*
woodcock 27, *27*
woodland
    after dark 28–31, *28–31*
    beech 20–23, *20–23*
    for dormice 85
    fungi 111–15, *111–15*
    New Forest 32–37, *32–37*
woodlark 36
woodlice 8, 105–6, *105–6*
    common (*Oniscus asellus*) 105
    Cylisticus convexus 105
    pill (*Armadillidium vulgare*) 106
    Platyarthus hoffmannseggi 106, *106*
wood mushroom (*Agaricus silvicola*) 114, *114*
woodpeckers 23, 101
    great spotted 35
woundwort, downy 17, *17*
wren 14, 15

Y
yarrow *18*
yellow bird's nest 22
yellowhammer 7

Acknowledgments

Photographs: Front cover Ardea, London/Johan de Meester, inset NHPA/Stephen Dalton; Back cover Natural Visions/Heather Angel; 1 NHPA/Stephen Dalton; 2-3 Ardea, London/David Dixon; 4(t) Bruce Coleman Ltd/Jane Burton, (b) Nature Picture Library/N Benvie; 5 Frank Lane Picture Agency/W Walker; 6(bl) NP/EA Janes, (bc) NP, (br) NP/Paul Sterry; 7(bl,bc) NP/Paul Sterry, (br) NP/EA Janes; 8(bl) NP/EA Janes, (bc,br) NP; 9(bl) NP/R Bush, (bc) NP, (br) NP/Paul Sterry; 10-11 Ardea, London/Chris Knights; 12(b) FLPA/M Nimmo, (b inset) NP/O Newman; 13(tr) FLPA/D Washington, (cl,br) NP/Paul Sterry; 14(tr) FLPA/AR Hamblin, (cru) OSF/Bob Gibbons, (cr) FLPA/M Hollings, (b) FLPA/M Clark; 15(tl,c) NP/Paul Sterry, (b) FLPA/R Tidman; 16(tc) NP/EA Janes, (br) NV; 16-17 NHPA/Laurie Campbell; 17(cr) NI, (br) BC/P.Clement; 18(tl) NV/Heather Angel, (tr) NP/Paul Sterry, (blu) BC/Kim Taylor, (bl) OSF/GI Bernard, (br) FLPA/T Hamblin; 19(tc) BC/WS Paton, (tr) NP/Paul Sterry, (b) FLPA/W.Walker; 20(c) NP/Paul Sterry; 21(b) FLPA/Ian Rose; 22(t) NP, (bl) NP; 23(tr) NP/Andrew Weston, (bl) NP/Andrew Cleave; 24(bl) Mike Read, (br) NP/D Osborn; 25(c) WW/S Austin, (br) NP/A Cleave; 26(tl) Windrush/G Langsbury, (tr) BC/G Dore, (bl) Windrush/J Gardner, (bc) Windrush/R Revels, (br) NP/P Green; 27(tl) Windrush/D Tipling, (tr) Windrush/R Revels, (b) FLPA/Derek Middleton; 28(r) NP/R Tidman, (bl) Ardea/M Watson; 29(tl) OSF/M Leach, (tr) OSF/Prestige Pictures, (cr) NSc/S Downer; 30(tl) OSF/M Leach, (tr) FLPA/Jurgen & Christine Sohns, (bl) BC/Jane Burton; 31(tl) OSF/I West, (tc) NSc/R Revels, (tr) OSF/K Atkinson, (b) NHPA/Stephen Dalton; 32 Mike Read; 33(tr) NHPA/Stephen Dalton, (cr) Mike Read; 34 Mike Read; 35 Mike Read; 36 Mike Read; 37(b) Mike Read; 38-39 Woodfall Wild Images/Bob Gibbons; 40(b) BC/Jane Burton; 41(tr) Aquila/S Downer, (b) NP/O Newman; 42(tr) Windrush/F Blackburn, (cl) NHPA/M Leach, (bl) FLPA/R Tidman; 43(br) NHPA/R Hosking; 44(tl, bl, br) OSF, (tr) Ardea; 45(tr) OSF/GI Bernard, (bl) NP/O Newman; 46 NHPA/Stephen Dalton; 47(tr) NHPA/J Hayward, (b) NSc/M Andera; 48(t) NP/M Andera; 49(tl) Ardea/JB & S Bottomley, (tr) OSF/B Watts, (bl) NP/Paul Sterry, (br) OSF/T Shepherd; 50(tl) NV/Heather Angel, (tr) OSF/B Watts, (bl) OSF/T Tilford; 51(tr) NP/Paul Sterry, (b) OSF; 52(r) BC/Kim Taylor, (bl) NHPA/A Rouse; 53(tr) BC/Kim Taylor, (b) Midsummer Books Ltd/P Bricknell; 54(t) Aquila/MC Wilkes, (b) NHPA/Stephen Dalton; 55(tl) BC/J van de Kam; 56(t) BC/G Langsbury, (cl) Mike Read, (c) NHPA/Andy Rouse, (cr) NP/R Tidman, (bl) Aquila/J Jones, (bc) BC/G Langsbury, (br) NP/EA Janes; 57(tl) NP/F Blackburn, (tr,bl) Mike Read; 58 FLPA/H Hautala; 59(tr) FLPA/M Jones, (b) BC/G McCarthy; 60(cr) David Chapman, (b) OSF/M Hamblin; 61(bl) Planet Earth Photos/PN Raven, (br) OSF/W Paton; 62(tl) NP/EA Janes, (cl,c,bc) BC, (cr) NSc/S Downer, (bl) OSF/DJ Cox, (br) FLPA/R Wilmhurst; 63(tl) OSF/M Hamblin, (c) FLPA/T Hamblin, (br) NSc/S Downer; 64 BC/F Labhardt; 65(tl) NP/Paul Sterry, (tr) BC/Jane Burton; 66(tl) OSF/B Watts, (tr) NP/Paul Sterry, (clu) OSF/T Shepherd, (blu) Ardea, (bl) Michael Chinery, (br) FLPA/GE Hyde; 67(tl) BC/F Sauer, (tr) BC/Jane Burton, (b) Ardea/C Knight; 68(tr) NP/NA Callow, (b) NV/Heather Angel; 69(tl) Ardea/B Gibbons, (cr) Ardea/JL Mason, (bl) Mihcael Chinery; 70(t) BC/Hans Reinhardt, (b) BC/J Jurka; 71(br) FLPA/D Cordier; 73(tl) BC/W Layer, (br) BC/Hans Reinhardt; 74 NP/Paul Sterry; 75(l) Andrew Gagg, (br) NV/Heather Angel; 78(tr) NP/Paul Sterry, (b) FLPA/A Wharton; 80(t,b) PW, (cu) FLPA/T Wharton, (c) NP/Paul Sterry; 81(t,cu,b) PW, (c) FLPA/E&D Hosking; 82(t) NP/EA Janes, (cu,c,b) PW; 83 Ardea, London; 84 NHPA/Stephen Dalton; 85(tr) FLPA/D Middleton, (c) NV/Heather Angel, (b) FLPA/V Gianotti; 86(tl) FLPA/H Clark, (bl) Michael Woods, (bcu) Ardea/P Morris, (bc) Ardea/Ian Beames, (br) Ardea/D Dixon; 87 NP/O Newman; 88 NP/SC Bisserot; 90(t,cu,c) NP/SC Bisserot, (b) NV/G Kinns; 91-92 NP/SC Bisserot; 93 BC/Hans Reinhardt; 94(tr) WW/J Robinson, (b) NP/N Bead; 95(tl) NHPA/DN Dalton, (tr) FLPA/E Hosking; 96(tl) Aquila/R Mills, (tc) BC/Kim Taylor, (tr) FLPA/M Jones, (cl) OSF/T Heath, (c) Windrush/D Tipling, (cr) FLPA/E Hosking, (br) FLPA/AR Hamblin; 97(tr) BC/K Wothe, (cl) NP/Paul Sterry, (b) FLPA/T Hamblin; 98(t) NHPA/R Tidman, (b) NP/H Clark; 99(t) NPL/G Dore, (b) NP/WS Paton; 100 NP/WS Paton; 101(cl) FLPA/Weiss, (c) Laurie Campbell, (cr) FLPA/E&D Hosking; 102(tc) NP/H Clark, (tr) Aquila, (cu) FLPA/E&D Hosking, (cru) FLPA/M Withers, (cr) Laurie Campbell, (bl) NP/WS Paton, (br) Laurie Campbell; 103(tr) Aquila, (c) BC/R Maier, (bl) BC/Jane Burton; 104 OSF/T Tipling; 105(t) NPL/N Benvie, (br) FLPA/D Jones; 106(tl) NP/Paul Sterry, (tr,cr) PW, FLPA/P Jones; 107(bl) OSF/W Cheng, (r) PW; 108(tl) NP/A Cleave, (c) FLPA/G Hyde, (cr) BC/P Clement, (br) FLPA/T Wharton; 109(tl) OSF/M Chillmaid, (tr) Ardea/B Gibbons, (bl) NHPA/N Callow, (br) PW; 110(tl,bl) PW, (tr) OSF, (bc) NPL/D McEwen; 111(tr) PW, (b) FLPA/Roger Wilmhurst; 113(t) NV/Heather Angel, (cu,c,b) PW; 114 PW; 115 PW; 116 NHPA/Laurie Campbell; 117(tl) NP/A Cleave, (c) Ecoscene/Gryniewicz, (b) OSF/R Packwood; 118(t) Ardea/GM Bahr, (cl) FLPA/D Grewock, (bl) OSF/London Scientific Films; 119(tr) WW/David Woodfall, (br) Ardea/B Gibbons; 120 Andrew Gagg; 121(cr) OSF/Bob Gibbons, (bl) NP/Paul Sterry; 122 NSc/W Cane; 123 NSc/R Revels; 124(cr) FLPA/D Hosking, (br) FLPA/R Wilmhurst.

Illustrations: 13(tr) Midsummer Books; 21(t), 25(t), 71-72, 76-77, 118-120, 122-125 Ian Garrard; 37 Rob Garard; 43, 48, 55, 60, 95, 101 John Ridyard; 79, 112 Wildlife Art Agency/Richard Bonson; 89 Wildlife Art Agency/Stuart Carter;

Key to Photo Library Abbreviations: BC = Bruce Coleman Ltd, FLPA = Frank Lane Photo Agency, NHPA = Natural History Photo Agency, NI= Natural Image, NP = Nature Photographers, NPL = Nature Picture Library, NSc = Natural Science Photos, NV = Heather Angel/Natural Visions, OSF = Oxford Scientific Films, PW = Premaphotos Wildlife, WW = Woodfall Wild.

Key to position abbreviations: b = bottom, bl = bottom left, blu = bottom left upper, br = bottom right, bru = bottom right upper, c = centre, cl = centre left, clu = centre left upper, cr = centre right, cru = centre right upper, cu = centre upper, l = left, r = right, sp = spread, t = top, tl = top left, tlu = top left upper, tr = top right, tru = top right upper.

Wildlife Watch
Grassland & Woodland in Autumn

Published by the Reader's Digest Association Limited, 2005

The Reader's Digest Association Limited
11 Westferry Circus, Canary Wharf
London E14 4HE

Reprinted 2007

We are committed to both the quality of our products and the service we provide to our customers, so please feel free to contact us on 08705 113366, or via our website at: www.readersdigest.co.uk

If you have any comments about the content of our books you can contact us at: gbeditorial@readersdigest.co.uk

® Reader's Digest, The Digest and the Pegasus logo are registered trademarks of The Reader's Digest Association, Inc., of Pleasantville, New York, USA

Reader's Digest General Books:
Editorial Director Julian Browne
Art Director Anne-Marie Bulat
Series Editor Christine Noble
Project Art Editor Julie Bennett
Prepress Accounts Manager Penelope Grose

This book was designed, edited and produced by Eaglemoss Publications Ltd, based on material first published as the partwork *Wildlife of Britain*

For Eaglemoss:
Project Editor Marion Paull
Editors Celia Coyne, Helen Spence, John Woodward
Art Editor Phil Gibbs
Editorial Assistant Helen Hawksfield
Consultant Jonathan Elphick
Publishing Manager Nina Hathway

Copyright © Eaglemoss Publications Ltd/Midsummer Books Ltd 2005

Printed and bound in Europe by Arvato Iberia

CONCEPT CODE: UK 0133/G/S
BOOK CODE: 630-00 UP0000-3
ISBN: 978 0 276 44055 7
ORACLE CODE: 356200008H.00.24